D0850190

THE SECOND TIME AROUND

Also by Leslie Aldridge Westoff

From Now to Zero: Fertility, Contraception, and Abortion in America (with Charles F. Westoff)

Leslie Aldridge Westoff

THE SECOND TIME AROUND

REMARRIAGE IN AMERICA

THE VIKING PRESS   NEW YORK

First published in 1977 by The Viking Press
625 Madison Avenue, New York, N.Y. 10022

Published simultaneously in Canada by The Macmillan Company of Canada
Limited

Library of Congress Cataloging in Publication Data

Westoff, Leslie Aldridge.
The second time around.

Includes index.
1. Remarriage—United States. I. Title.
HO536.W45   301.42'7   76–49532
ISBN 0–670–62834–4

Printed in the United States of America

Set in Videocomp Times Roman

For C. F. W.

Acknowledgments

I would like to doff my hat to all my husbands, their current and former wives and girl friends, my many stepchildren, and my friends who have made up the background of my experience and helped me realize the need for this book.

Thanks to the editors of *The New York Times Magazine* for stimulating my interest in this book by accepting the original article on which it is based.

Thanks to my editor, Barbara Burn, for her particularly incisive comments and excellent suggestions, but even more importantly for her encouragement and very personal enthusiasm.

Thanks to my son, Geoffrey, who thinks it's great that I can work on a typewriter with only two fingers and get something done and who has lived through the changes in our lives so well.

Thanks too to my husband's son, David, and daughter, Carol Sahlman, who provoked me into thinking about what was happening to all of us by just reacting.

Thanks to Allison Hankinson, who typed a portion of the manuscript and freed my hands to write.

And warm thanks to my husband Charles F. Westoff whose mania for achievement, whose passion for facts, and whose joy in life provided a constant impetus for work.

Contents

THE SECOND TIME AROUND

THE RISE
AND FALL
OF MARRIAGE

1

If they hurried, they could make the drive up from Virginia through the snaking mountain roads and soft green valleys and still arrive home before dark. But first they had a stop to make.

They parked the loaded station wagon just off the cool, leafy roadway. As they entered the red brick church, their steps sounded a loud staccato. They walked alone down the long narrow aisle. There were no smiling guests, no weeping parents, no resounding sounds of organ music, no excited attendants, no flowers, no veils, nothing borrowed or blue, old or new. There were only vacant seats and the towering vaults of empty space, flooded for the moment with shafts of sunlight.

The minister was young, in fact younger than they. And quite uneasy. The man and woman about to be married were impatient to be off. "Could we begin now and consummate the nuptials?" the man asked awkwardly, trying to use the vocabulary of traditional formality. It wasn't at all what he meant to say. And the minister's face colored and he fumbled nervously. The whole situation was more comic than real—a dress rehearsal in which the action was happening to other people. The couple had been living together for some time.

They had each been through marriage before, and the seas were charted. Ceremony had little to do with how they were feeling. They wanted to have this necessary interruption over with and get on with the job of living.

At about this same moment in a small New Jersey suburb, a man, whose wife had died a year earlier, and a woman, whose divorced husband still lived in the same neighborhood, stood before a judge in the town hall waiting for him to marry them. The woman, who had already moved into the man's house with her two teen-age girls, had brought them along. The man's teen-age son could not be present because he was in bed with the flu. It is just as well that he could not come, thought the woman, realizing how ill at ease the boy might feel. Although each had many friends in this small town, only the couple who were acting as witnesses had been invited. The woman wore a dress that she considered appropriate. "You look so matronly, Mom," her girls had remarked. The man wore a blue business suit that he had worn many times before. After the ceremony, they all went home. Several days later they would write his mother to say that they were about to be married, not getting the chronology quite right because they had not found time to write sooner and they didn't want to hurt her. The woman had never met her new mother-in-law.

In countless cities and towns all over the country, similar scenes are being played out. Would a second (or third) marriage for these couples be better or worse than their first marriages? It could go either way, for remarriage, like any other personal relationship, is a mixed bag of pros and cons. There are the great moments—and the hassles. But one thing is certain: for better or worse remarriage has begun and will continue to be dramatically different than first marriage.

Facts and Myths

Old-fashioned, once-in-a-lifetime, till-death-do-us-part marriage may be going on the rocks these days, but remarriage has been booming. Divorce rates are soaring. Couples are breaking up like icebergs in a summer sea. Demographers report that more than a million people get divorced every year. This means that one out of every three couples decides to divorce sooner or later. Although our marriage rate appeared to be rising to counteract this destruction of existing marriages, until a few years ago, when it suddenly dropped, this rising rate was no more than a mirage. Our first-marriage rate has actually been *falling* for the last thirty years and what has buoyed up the figures has been remarriage. Every year, four out of five people who split up will remarry. As far as marriages are concerned, one out of every four is now usually a second, sometimes a third marriage, occasionally even a fourth. Only a small proportion of these involve widowed persons.

These second marriages are known as "blended families," or "reconstituted families," and with their complicated cross-currents of relationships, they are quite different from the nuclear families produced by first marriages. Unfortunately, little is known about second marriages—despite the sociologists, psychologists, and popular media waiting to pounce on anything new. There was a flurry of investigation in the 1950s, but no significant research has been done on the subject. It is shocking to find that there is almost nothing current, nothing in the journals or popular press to guide the average person or his psychiatrist or marriage counselor.

In a recent conversation with Mrs. Belle Parmet, a psychiatric social worker from New Jersey, she remarked on this astounding culture lag. She told me that she had attended a regional meeting of family therapists at which many counselors were gathered for several days of discussion. She said, "I sat there during the whole time listening to talks about THE family, studies of THE family, arguments about THE family, until I couldn't stand it any longer. I got up and said, 'What on earth do you mean . . . THE family? There is no such thing. There are two-parent families, one-parent families, no-parent families, three- or four-parent families, families without children.' There was a burst of applause when I finished."

This experience illustrates the incredible fact that many psychiatrists and counselors have been slow in recognizing the vital changes that have taken place in the family, in doing research on these changes, and in writing about them. The family can no longer be thought of as a neat, encapsulated entity, simple and easily definable. Mrs. Parmet said, "We have been taught to think of family as the biological family (parents and children related by blood ties). Well, that's not *the* family any longer. That's only *one* kind of family." She went on to lament that "there's very little written in the field. We have no guidelines. The culture hasn't institutionalized these new forms of the family yet."

Sociologists have concentrated on more flamboyant developments, such as cohabitation on the nation's campuses, and have largely ignored the growing phenomenon of remarriage. Marriage counselors say they have been so busy counseling that they simply have not taken time to study their cases. There has been an endless stream of articles and books on marriage and divorce, mainly divorce, and there the story stops. No one has adequately followed people who survive divorce, as most do, and tracked them on into their second marriages. Remarriage has always been sketchily dealt with. If the victims of divorce can be shown the tricks of how to grow strong and rebuild their lives, most writers then leave them drifting off into the sunset in this newfound state. What really happens to them afterward has never been properly pursued.

The U.S. Census Bureau has provided some of the basic facts: 75 per cent of all marriages are first marriages, 20 per cent are second marriages, and 6 per cent are third marriages. Most divorced people tend to marry other divorced people. Most remarry soon, within an average of three years. And most choose August rather than June for the wedding. The average age at first marriage is twenty-one for women and twenty-four for men; the averages at second marriages are twenty-five for women, and thirty for men. Women wait (or are kept waiting) longer than men before remarrying. Up to age twenty-four, divorced men and women have the same chance of remarrying. But from age twenty-five to forty-four, the number of divorced men remarrying is almost double that of divorced women. And from forty-five to sixty-four, men remarry two and a half times more than do women—all of which would argue for a woman's leaving a bad marriage as soon as possible! More men remarry because their pool of potential wives covers an age range from young girls up to their own age level; but for most women, the choice is limited to the small number of available men in their own age bracket or older. For some reason, probably related to the egocentric male and his image of machismo, younger men rarely marry older women—they usually prefer to be sought after by younger women, those who represent the symbols of glamourous youth, more like nymphs than aging mothers.

Except for the woman with a graduate degree, the more education the individual has and the higher the income, the greater the chance of remarriage. Women with higher degrees have probably become more interested in careers than marriage and don't choose it so often. Some of the elements that were expected by the experts to have lowered the divorce rate, but obviously didn't, are rising ages for marriage (more stable marriages occur later), less poverty, and an increasing proportion of adults with a college education. (Are better-educated people really supposed to be better able to live with each other?) That has come to be one of the myths connected with remarriage, for the divorce rate has not yet dipped. Marriage later in life and more education and money have only served to help people feel more independent.

And this leads to the next myth of remarriage, one that has been around so long it has been set to music. Love is supposed to be better the second time around and second marriages must therefore be better than first marriages. All this may be true. Love may be lovier, the marriage may be better, but couples are still vulnerable to the problems of living with another person, the unbelievable complexities of trying to make two families into one, as well as the problems inherent in the institution of marriage itself. It is not a foolproof relationship —neither the first nor the second time. Remarriage is obviously not *all* good or *all* bad. It is some of each, though one might, and I will later, compare the *quality* of the "good" and the *quality* of the "bad" and find the "good" better the second time and the "bad" not so bad. However, the myth that second marriages are better and more successful must be qualified: they *may* be better, but, nevertheless, a higher proportion of second marriages fail than first marriages. They are statistically no more successful than first marriages. They are, in fact, slightly less so. Dr. Paul Glick, senior demographer at the U.S. Census Bureau, predicted in June 1975 that if things continue as they have, in addition to the 36 per cent of first marriages that end in divorce (a little over one in three), 40 per cent of second marriages will also dissolve.

Dr. Glick conjectures that one reason why many second marriages also fail is that remarrying couples have already been through one divorce and, consequently, will not hesitate to divorce again, if necessary—a kind of practice effect or learning experience. Second divorces, he believes, screen out the spoiled, the immature, and the less disciplined, some of whom are unable to live continuously with another person and perhaps should not be married at all. As each marriage becomes successful for those who made an earlier mistake, the proportion still failing will include more and more of the problem people. It's a sort of reverse panning-for-gold effect. By the third or fourth panning, those who are left are the chronically discontent and those people who may even find it difficult to live with themselves. As might be expected, second marriages ending in divorce do not last as long as first ones. The average duration of those that can't make it the second time is five years compared to the well-known seven-year itch of first marriages.

Why So Many Divorces?

Never before in history have there been so many divorces or remarriages. Something very profound seems to be shaking our traditional concepts of what a marriage is, or is supposed to be. Always frowned upon in the past, divorce has only recently become an accepted part of American life. As Jane Spock, the seventy-year-old wife of Dr. Benjamin Spock, put it in an interview in *The New York Times* on the occasion of the breakup of their forty-eight-year-old marriage: "I would have spoken up before but women just didn't do those things then. Instead of getting good and angry, you went into the other room and cried. . . . I wasn't able to come out and say what I thought because I thought it was wiser not to. In those days you got into trouble with your marriage if you did." Today she could and did speak up.

One reason why there are so many remarriages in our society is that it is now so easy for first marriages to break up. Liberal, no-fault divorce laws have lightened some of the economic burden on the man in a divorce, so that remarriage is becoming more financially feasible —though it's still a tough struggle supporting two families instead of one. Second, because of increasing education and the declining importance of older religious and traditional values, divorce has simply become more socially acceptable, and, in some circles, even fashionable. The advent of the women's rights movement and consciousness-raising (sitting on the floor with a group of friends and telling each other what's really bothering you) have undoubtedly influenced the woman's view of marriage. Today she is no longer satisfied by the children and security which her mother settled for. The feminist movement has been so vocal that it has resulted in legitimizing women's hitherto unrecognized, or at least unexpressed, emotional and intellectual needs. With the opening up of the job market to give women greater opportunity and independence, with an increased emphasis on the individual and on encountering the inner self—of saying, feeling, doing what one wishes—women's expectations in marriage have risen. Both partners, in fact, demand something positive and worthwhile out of a relationship, a more compatible and intimate bond than the strange, impersonal, nagging marriage that many of our parents accepted. A woman who might have hung on to marriage with desperation is now much more willing to split a relationship that isn't working or a marriage that falls short of some ideal.

Even the formerly conservative worlds of business, with corporation manners, and politics, with voter-consciousness, now sanction matrimonial switches, which not so long ago meant the instant demise of a once-promising career. Vice-President Rockefeller barely made it under the wire when he divorced and remarried at the time when the moral climate began to change. In the 1970s, a breath of fresh air swept in new attitudes toward behavior which have affected many areas of our lives. There has been a loosening of religious strictures, and of rigid social and moralistic judgments. People are more relaxed, less uptight, more apt to tell each other what they really think. Children have become more independent of their parents. Women have become more independent of men. Formality is vanishing, and the social rules are being modified. Instead of doing what they think they *ought* to do, people are doing what they *want* to do, or, as they like to call it, their own thing. There is a strong sense of equality in the family, where everyone is beginning to carry the same weight. Now men and women are telling each other for the first time, as honestly as they can, what they want out of life. They are sharing dreams that see through and go beyond the romantic illusions (nurtured for so long by Hollywood and popular fiction) with which we blindly plunged into our often superficial and flimsy first marriages.

But most marriages in this country were not made during these last few expressive years and do not benefit from current attitudes. Imposing the new freedoms on an old marriage has in many instances led to a great deal of friction. The once sought-after traditional marriage, which still exists and which has shaped American society for ages—

the picket fences and silver patterns and for better or worse, is now beginning to look more like the result of an outmoded idea which never really worked as well as it was supposed to—although everyone pretended it did.

On the other hand, now that divorce can be obtained more easily and men and women have more opportunity to live alone, remarry, or choose careers, they have more reason to re-evaluate their lives and ask themselves, "Am I really happy?" There is an increasing self-consciousness about happiness, though. For every freedom there is a price to pay. The freedom we have won is the chance for a more diverse and interesting life. The price is an increased dissatisfaction with what we have, a restlessness spawned by the many options open to us. We are the victims of what one well-known sociologist, who happens to be my third husband, calls "marital hypochondria." We are becoming more concerned with the health of our marriages. As in the past, for example, the field of medicine had few cures, and people expected to be sick and die young. Today, with all the possibilities of prevention, cure, treatment, and transplant, we have developed an obsession about health and longevity—and it may be the same with marriage. There is a lot of similar public and private soul-searching going on, and all kinds of alternatives for every marital sickness.

The Rush to Be Interviewed

This book, then, is about why people marry, what happens to them as they travel along through marriage, how they struggle to keep from being submerged by circumstances—as though marriage moved them with its own momentum, dragging them along after it, leaving them often not knowing what they are supposed to want or do. It is about divorce and the time of awakening that follows, but mainly it is about remarriage, and what goes into a remarriage. What makes it work.

Some generalizations are offered. But since this is a journalistic inquiry and not a sociological study, though the two often overlap each other's domains, there are obviously not going to be any claims made that the majority of people in the country think this way or that. There is little such information available. So, for every generalization, there may be readers who are exceptions, and for them, an experience may have been totally different. I am merely reporting what the middle-class trends appear to be to a journalist who has spent many long but fascinating hours interviewing men, women, and children who have all gone through divorce and most through remarriage. It was remarkable to me, in view of the complexities of life and the broad range of personality and need, how very similar their stories were. The details varied: some people had no children or two children; some had money troubles and some managed well. But despite the differences in circumstances, the main impact of divorce and remarriage seems strikingly the same for everyone. I was profoundly struck by the fact that, despite their living in different geographic areas and having different occupations, experience is treating them all the same way. Things were hurting with a hurt that was universally recognizable, or they were being euphoric with a happiness that seemed to blow across the country like a prevailing wind. At moments I had the eerie feeling that in all these interviews, in all these places, I was talking to the same person.

At first I wondered why—with different upbringings and different aspirations and different husbands and different children—the experience would have impressed them in precisely the same way; people had always seemed so different from each other. Then I was forced to conclude that no matter how different all the superficialities of life, the external aspects, people are frighteningly, startlingly similar. Almost all had the same responses. There were one or two who didn't fit, but the overwhelming proportion did, as though they had come from the same mold. They were all speaking the same lines. For example, when I mentioned the word Divorce, most people unhesitatingly replied Bitter. Children—Manipulative. Remarriage—Mature, Aware. Ex-Spouse—Guilt. New Spouse—In Tune, Commitment.

Although those I interviewed were not picked as a scientific random sample of thousands, nor were they superficially interrogated via the questionnaires of professional pollsters, the hours of extremely personal face-to-face discussions make the impressions recorded in this book plausible. For in something as complex as remarriage, there are no simple yes-and-no answers. There are shades of black and white and gray, intensities of problem, degrees of solution, and levels of happiness. I am grateful to all those who allowed me to walk with them through the private landscapes of their lives and share their most intimate feelings. I found it remarkable that so many people were willing, even anxious to talk about their painful personal sentiments.

Almost no one refused to talk to me, except one or two who hoped to write their own stories. For the rest, I was given many hours of people's precious time, schedules were shifted to accommodate me—almost to the point where I felt pursued. Several who obviously had little time because they were on the verge of trips insisted on seeing me.

Why? Why do people want to talk about what has happened to them? About remarriage? I can only surmise that it is because people are flattered by the fact that someone is so interested in them; they have perhaps never had anyone sit down with them and go over the whole story of what happened, and they have always harbored the need to talk about it; they want to understand even more about themselves; and they want to know what is happening to others. In recent years when remarriages have been multiplying in such great numbers, their relative newness in the great social network has left people a bit unsettled, confused. Many told me they had no one to talk to about remarriage during the years when they considered and then opted for it. There was nothing to read that could give them a clue as to what they could expect or what had happened to others; they never knew whether what was happening to them was unusual or normal; they didn't know quite how to respond to or how to handle all the new situations; their world was utterly different than it had been before, they knew that, but how was everybody else in their same situation behaving?

People asked me what others had said and what conclusions I had reached. One woman looked at me after our interview and said she was extremely anxious to find out something about other people's observations: "It would help so much to know my experience is not unique." They all wanted to be involved in the investigation so that when it was finished they could examine it and their own part in it, and know a lot more about the new life-style of remarriage than was possible before.

I talked to people from New York to Honolulu. Their occupations ranged from male minister to female politician to housewife. There were travel agents, executives, doctors, secretaries, administrators, accountants, singers, saleswomen. I did not attempt to reach children below high school age, since I felt this might harm them more than it might clarify things for them and me. The only stipulations in all the interviews was that they would be completely confidential and that case histories would not be so obvious that anyone would be immediately recognizable to his or her friends. Nevertheless, it is very likely that, because of the incredible similarities in people's experiences, readers may instantly "recognize" the stories of people I have never met. This will only testify to the universality of what befalls us, and it should not be assumed that the story I tell is meant to be, in fact, a particular story. I hope those in a remarriage will read and understand what is happening to them and that those in a first marriage will perhaps learn enough from others' experience to better their first marriages, or to take heart in ending them if that seems inevitable. They will, in any case, know more of what it's all about.

The Downfall of Our Upbringing

When parents raise their children to the time that they go off to college, they assume that kids will have observed enough, soaked up enough of the virtues around them through osmosis, if not discussion, to prepare them to lead exemplary lives. They have, after all, come from good, middle-class homes. They will have the right values. Yet one of the startling revelations was that literally every man and woman I spoke to mentioned that the upbringing they had had left much to be desired. It was almost a mass condemnation of parents. One woman said: "My mother is one of those people who shouldn't have had kids. We were always in her way." Another told me, "My parents were repressed. They did what people thought they should do. My mother was a cold fish. She wanted to be warm, but she didn't know how to be."

"I had no concept of marriage other than the bad marriage my parents had," said one person I talked to. "I always assumed I'd have a better one, but that assumption was bound up in romantic notions of houses in Connecticut with big stone fireplaces. I had no sense of what was needed in a day-to-day relationship, what one did when differences arose. Why should I? In my romanticized dream there would be no differences. It all seemed like one eternal date where he would not have to go home at night. I suppose I dreamt up this ideal in reaction to my parents' empty relationship. If anything at all happened between them, it was behind closed doors."

A recently remarried college administrator said: "Neither family, church, Boy Scouts, nor school made me remotely aware of things that affected my life, skills, or preparation for marriage. I knew nothing about relating to women, the demands of sex, or child-rearing. I had to face most of the major things in my life just winging it by trial and error. I had my head in the sand. I am angry that those needs were things one didn't talk about and I couldn't articulate them. They weren't subjects that were appropriate. We weren't taught to think about them. There was a vast sea of deliberate insensitivity. I am resentful that I didn't wake up earlier."

Sex, in particular, seems to be one subject that was never discussed in the family. Parents who were ignorant about it, feared it, or were embarrassed by it, hid the whole subject as though it were immoral, something that nice boys and girls didn't think about. Thus growing children were left, and still are, to muddle through this delicate area unaided, developing some pretty difficult sexual hang-ups of their own, problems that often remain as insurmountable barriers in their later marriages.

One woman said: "My mother felt, when it came to sex, that anything below the waist was not to be discussed . . . and she didn't feel too comfortable with things above the waist, either."

"I had a very proper upbringing," said another woman. "We never talked about sex or marriage. My parents were unhappy themselves but maintained a façade, so I was always getting mixed messages about what marriage was."

A man told me: "In my family we never mentioned the word sex. I still don't know if my parents ever had any, except for the one time they must have to produce me."

All my informants said they had received no training, no information, no discussion (either at home or at school) that could possibly prepare them for marriage. Because they had been so intimidated by their parents' problems and behavior and so protected from what really was happening, many felt they had simply not known much about personal relationships. How did their parents solve disagreements, create excitement in their lives, spend private hours together, decide on how to spend money? Did they make love? Did each know what was bothering the other? What kind of giving and taking was necessary? No one had told them. The private walls were too high. Children were expected to be interested only in eating and playing and doing well in school. And when they grew up, all those I interviewed lamented—to the point of anger and resentment—their ignorance and inexperience the first time they married. When it came to marriage, they held a crazy set of expectations that had nothing to do with reality. It is sobering to reflect that a boy or girl growing up within the context of marriage, surrounded by it for seventeen years, enveloped by it during the period when he or she learns all about life, given two married people as parents, would have so little notion of what a marriage is or what it entails. Our small nuclear families are not too small to be sealed off from any intimacy, each person suffering with the lonely knowledge of his own private frustrations. Ought we not communicate with the people closest to us, those we care about most? Why the reticence to expose children to problems or bring unpleasantness out into the open or talk about sexual needs? For the generation brought up on the aftereffects of Victorian sensibility and insensitivity, of repressed emotion, perhaps this was the only way to do it. One of the things that differentiates us from the last few generations is of course that they had fewer options open to them in life, and therefore less preparation for marriage was needed. If marriage for a woman in the past meant pleasing one's husband, raising children, baking bread, and, above all, being an obedient wife, one could far more easily prepare for the role than one can prepare for the concept of the liberated wife.

But even today younger mothers seem to undermine their children's chances for a good marriage in the future by producing men who will be spoiled, who will never grow up because no one has encouraged them to do so. They, too, seem overindulged, protected from reality, as though they exist as love objects for their mothers. And girls are not brought up in any special way, are taught to be neither housewives nor mothers nor career-seekers. They seem to be allowed to drift whichever way the tide of chance and their own whims take them. Their egos are not strong: they have no sense of driving purpose. Daddy loves them and gives them money for clothes, but not much more. The confusion of pressures felt by growing girls is evident. One woman told me: "My parents wanted me to go through college and prepare for a career only as insurance. They really expected me to get married and not work."

It is interesting that a recent study—a $30-million project of the federal government*—tested a half million students over the last six years and found that the males outrank the females in academic achievement, particularly in math, science, social studies, and citizenship. It concluded that the woman's achievement drops because of the "subtle and not-so-subtle forces—both within the education system and society in general—that affect female education and achievement." The females are found to be fairly equal to males until age nine. By age thirteen, though, females have begun a decline that continues through adulthood.

The "not-so-subtle forces" in society must mean, among other things, the image of the female role that girls get from their mothers and fathers and from the marriages their parents project. Women are definitely made to feel like less important individuals, at least they have been in the past, and they have come to believe it. One woman revealed her sense of inferiority when she remarked: "I had the idea that if something went wrong in our marriage, it was my fault. That I should alter my behavior, I should be the one to change. And I couldn't."

It seems to me that a marriage between a spoiled man, who has learned to feel superior, who expects everything to be done for him, and who expects to make all the rules himself, and a confused woman, who has seen her mother struggle with an inferior position in life, who has seen herself taken less than seriously by teachers in school, who has been encouraged by them to study art history or music instead of math or science, whose sports and academic needs have always been placed second to a boy's needs, is going to have problems. A college student to whom I spoke told me that in high school as recently as 1973 her chemistry teacher tried to talk her out of going into engineering, and when she told her counselor she was interested in the sciences and asked him what he recommended, his answer was home economics. This counselor also taught mechanical drawing and refused to allow her to take his course. I wondered how many such put-downs a girl could take and still care enough to fight back. I wonder how many such put-downs she can take both in school and in the family and still come out in a position to pick up her share of a marriage commitment.

*Conducted by the National Assessment of Education Progress, Dr. Roy H. Forbes, Director, Denver, Colorado.

Along with all this lack of direction, children have also been brought up with the idea that divorce is not really right. So if stuck with a bad marriage the first time, they have been expected to hang on and make the best of it. They have inherited the idea that divorce is somehow shameful, and a sign of failure.

"When I was a girl," said a recently remarried woman, "my good old-fashioned Catholic mother told me, 'Don't you play with that little girl, her mother is a divorcée.' "

A man said: "I was reluctant to tell my parents. I was the first in my family to get a divorce."

Why Marry the First Time?

Visions of marriage are veiled by fantasy and parents' inadequacies as marriage partners are strongly felt, but, nevertheless, men and women do marry. And not only do most people get married knowing nothing about marriage and not being ready for it, but almost all I interviewed felt they had been much too young when they got married.

The reasons that people marry vary according to what kind of marriage it is, first or second. Reasons for second marriages are quite different from reasons for the first. Most couples told me they first married because of social pressure, because society is geared to couples and if you weren't part of a couple you were out of it. Or they married because their friends were marrying, or they wanted to live with someone after getting sexually involved. Some wanted to escape from their parents, others were simply feeling the pressures of age. Making a mistake, most agreed, was so easy that it was almost inevitable.

The father of four children said: "I believe my first marriage was an almost completely automatic act, the thing I was supposed to do after I graduated from college. Something that was expected of me at that point in my life." Another person said: "I married because it was a disgrace not to be married in the 1960s. It was suspect. There is more support now for the way you want to live."

"I got married to escape my parents and home," a woman told me. "There was no other way to do it, economically. I couldn't earn enough. I was eighteen the first time. It was so much of a game."

A man reported: "Lots of my friends slept with a girl and then felt obligated to marry her. It had just been a whim to begin with; I doubt if they were in love."

"The first time I married I didn't think," said a young woman. "I had no concerns about getting married, having children, or a career. I was just out of college one day and down the aisle the next."

"The reason why I married is very simple," a woman remembered. "My parents and society told me, 'A woman isn't complete until she's caught her man.'"

And another person admitted: "If any discussion had ever gone on about marriage, not so much with my parents but with my peers, the kind of discussion people have in college today, I'd have not married. I'd have waited."

People who are remarried today, then, married the first time essentially because they thought they were *supposed* to marry. It was the next step along the road after college, which they had left laden with academic degrees and emotional gaps. They were full of square roots and the meaning of the *Odyssey* and how to say "snowed-in" in French and what the gross national product means, but had absolutely no knowledge of what would be needed in dealing with people. A calculator would help with square roots, but what would help with people? Where they were supposed to connect to others, they were raw and unfinished. Given their upbringing, there was no way they could have known whether they were making an obvious mistake or a good compatible choice.

Is It Real Love?

The things that draw people together the first time, attracting them to such a degree that they think they want to live together for life, are clearly very different at the beginning than they are later in life. In a first marriage, we imagine we're in love when our stomachs clutch, we lose our appetite, and we think that's *it.* But is it? Do we initially mistake feelings of emotional excitement and pleasure as love? How can people be in love at first sight? In a poll conducted at several universities, college students were asked what one thing they most wished they knew about romantic love. A surprisingly large number of them replied that they wanted to know how they could tell when they were really in love and when they were just infatuated. Ellen Berscheid, a psychologist at the University of Minnesota, and Elaine Walster,* a sociologist at the University of Wisconsin, suggest that the difference may just be a matter of semantics, with people using romantic love to signify a love that is in progress, while infatuation may be referring to a love that has passed. "If a relationship flowers," they say, "one continues to believe he is experiencing true love; if a relationship dies, one concludes that he was merely infatuated. . . . In our culture, romantic love seems to be the *sine qua non* for marriage."

What are the things that make people think they are in love and eventually lead to a first marriage? Drs. Berscheid and Walster tell about a "computer dance" that was staged for college freshmen. All the men and women who signed up for the dance were paired randomly, each girl with a taller man. Questionnaires were given out at intermission to determine how well the pairs had hit it off and why. The study showed that "the *only* apparent determinant of how much each person liked his or her date, how much he or she wanted to see the partner again, and [it was later determined] how often the man actually did ask his partner for subsequent dates, was simply [and get this] how physically attractive the partner was. The more physically attractive the date, the more he or she was liked. Every effort to find additional factors which might possibly predict attraction failed." Brighter or more socially adept students were not liked any better than less accomplished or interesting students, as long as they were attractive.

Physical attractiveness is obviously a shaky basis for a lifetime relationship. It is even ludicrous. One ought to find one's partner attractive in a good marriage, but the dozens of other more important qualities should come first—if for no other reason than that looks don't last. If this is true, and it certainly must be true in many instances, it is not surprising that marriages are breaking up at such a rapid pace. Marriages, even in the recent past, seem to involve well-intentioned, young, attractive people who obviously don't know enough to make conscious choices. They don't even think in such terms. They react against parents; they are attracted by sex, beauty,

*"Physical Attractiveness," Ellen Berscheid and Elaine Walster, in *Advances in Experimental Social Psychology,* Leonard Berkowitz, ed., Vol. 7 (New York: Academic Press, Inc. 1974).

and what everyone else is doing. They fall into marriage; and then try to make it work. Even today, with much more talk about sex and marriage, with much more living together before marriage, mistakes are still being made for the same old reasons.

The response of young people may in part be a product of the powerful sales campaigns, long used by Hollywood and Madison Avenue, to promote everything that's sold in this country from movies to toothpaste—romance. "If he kisses you once will he kiss you again?" Yes, of course, if you use the right toothpaste, if you get the ring around his collar off, if you smoke the right cigarette. While in the past we were enticed by the image of some tall, dark and handsome man crushing in his arms a beautiful, perhaps smart—it was hard to tell since she was always playing dumb—but always docile woman, now we simply have no romantic models to follow. There is the handsome Redford, but there are the equally popular Brando and Savalas. There is the beautiful Dunaway, but there are the not-so-beautiful Streisand and Minnelli. Romance today means being saved from an earthquake, a skyscraper, an inferno, or the devil himself. We mix our romance with horror, cataclysm, or violence and nothing is ever said about the basic reasons that people have for being in love, which would, perversely, be unromantic. Meanwhile, we are not completely liberated from old-fashioned notions of romance thanks to the never-ending stream of old movie revivals on television. These, and our lingering memories of childhood adventure tales, still manage to color our consciousness.

A woman in her twenties complained: "My first marriage grew out of hopelessness. How do I change my position in life? I had to pretend to myself I was in love and it was going to be permanent. I had the old romantic conceptions. I even cried at my own wedding. In six months I was looking at other men."

A very attractive remarried man, who had worked in the foreign service, said wryly: "My divorce really started three months after I got married. She had romanticized marriage to such an extent, it could never live up to what she wanted."

"I used to think of marriage romantically," a dark-haired woman said. "My first husband played the cello. He looked beautiful. I became infatuated. When he put down the cello, I couldn't bear it."

A chemist put it quite simply: "At the beginning, people can be attracted to each other for relatively trivial reasons. But after the first few years, the romantic sexual thrill wears off." Then, of course, people are stuck with what's left.

What Went Wrong?

And so, despite the faulty upbringing, the romantic illusions, the untried youth, the ridiculous expectations, people got married. Then, through chance, through the mutual ability to learn quickly and adjust, through dumb luck, many of the marriages worked. Some people really loved each other and some learned to. Others just decided to grin and bear it, that one person was as good as another. But one-third of them didn't. And who knows how many other marriages are sour, are fermenting, and continue because of inertia; because it's just too much trouble to undo all the shared responsibilities, mutual obligations, and hopelessly entwined lives. People stay together unhappily because the man worries about who will do his laundry (a cliché, but true) and cook for him, or because the woman is afraid if she gives up this marriage, no matter how bad, she may not find another husband. And in her mind, a bad marriage is better than no marriage. How many stay married because they worry about what their children or neighbors will think? Or their family? How many stay married for religious reasons? How many stay married because they fear uncertainty? A marriage is a familiar setting in which to live, no matter how awful it may have become. It is secure: he brings home money; she keeps house. They both have a comfortable place to eat and sleep, and material things are available. The frightening unknowns can be ignored and one does the best one can, without any conscious love or closeness. After all, there are many people who think that this is the fate of all long-term marriages. I imagine that if all bad marriages were to dissolve, there would be at least double the present number of divorces.

As women become more daring, truly assert themselves as people, find jobs that can support them, and living alone becomes an acceptable way of life, more women will divorce; they will have decided that it's worth taking the chance of finding something better than what one had. Going through a period of uncertainty and loneliness may be worth it.

People who later remarried looked back and saw how bad things were in their first marriages:

"In my first marriage, we woke up one day and just realized we were both different and wanted different things. We realized we hadn't really known each other when we married."

"In my first marriage we were both unhappy, just staggering along."

"I wanted the divorce because I wasn't happy. Our marriage counselor said, 'I've never seen people so unable to communicate as you.' "

"It takes courage to separate. I suppose I could just have gone on. He wanted to go on. It was convenient for him to stay married to me. I cooked his meals and did the laundry. I was pleasant. I stayed on because the kids were small and there was no money. A few of my friends got divorced. I finally got very angry at something he did. I was suddenly finished with the marriage. I realized that, in his mind, he came first. I was nothing."

Another person told me her marriage broke up because "both of us were spoiled and immature. There was a lack of communication. Neither of us knew how to go about opening it up. If we had a disagreement, I'd withdraw, and he'd go away on a business trip. We avoided having to face the problem. But we wouldn't have known what to do anyway."

And one woman said quite frankly: "We were unsuited to each other. I was more intelligent than he. I knew life could be better than that. I knew there must be a man somewhere I could have a better relationship with."

Her remark, made on a sunny day out West, caused me to stop and wonder how many women, supposed to be less accomplished and less intelligent than their husbands, but who are not, are still playing the role of the inferior female? How many are not saying what they think for fear it will overshadow a husband's remarks, or humiliate him? It must be a lifelong habit of many women to hold themselves back, to understate, to remain in the background as they push their husbands forward, very much as their husbands' mothers must have done. I was delighted to meet one woman who admitted she was smart and who wanted a man she could meet on her own level.

There was a torrent of other points made about first-marriage breakups. One was sexual incompatibility. "When it broke up," said a woman, "he told me our sex hadn't been good and said it was my fault." Another put-down for a woman? Or maybe a series of put-downs and a lack of guidance had made her into a frigid, tense person who could not enjoy sex.

People often grow apart, not unexpectedly. A man suggested: "When you're twenty-four and you try to imagine what your feelings about life will be at forty-five, you can't. The things you value at twenty-four change. If you can get through divorce, you have a chance to make a marriage as the new person you are."

Some find communication difficult. If they cannot talk to each other, one wonders if they were not strangers to begin with. Others are literally afraid of their spouse's temper, and just don't talk about certain sensitive subjects. Some people develop different goals. Some finally realize that the person they married is not the person they thought they married. Hopes and dreams of success which never come to fruition may make people dissatisfied with their spouse. Some discover that people on dates are not the same as people at home. They may break up because a wife decides to go out and work and have a career which her husband can't accept. Some may discover that being a couple in love was one thing but being parents of omnipresent children is another, and that family life has eroded the marriage. There are innumerable reasons for dissatisfaction with the first marriage, none of them surprising, given the lack of any marriage preparation.

In a survey done in a New Jersey suburb, it was found that the two main causes for family breakup were alcohol and women's frustrated career ambitions. In other words, women wanted "out" of the traditional marriage in which they were valued as housewives, a role which many men still believe is all they really need in their marriage partner. And so the women left, and more and more women are doing the same. Frequently, of course, the decision to divorce is not mutual. Often one member of the partnership wants to leave and the other is helpless to prevent it. The National Council on Family Relations estimates that about four of every ten couples who are divorced include one member who did not want it. In six of ten cases, they both want it.

Whatever the reasons for breaking up the first marriage, divorce is not going to be very pleasant. It may well be the most difficult time of one's life, something each spouse is as equally unfit to deal with as the couple was in dealing with marriage in the first place. And other people may not be of much help to the pair at this time. As Dr. Berscheid told me: "Social science doesn't even understand the basis on which marriages are initiated, so, understandably, the dynamics of their disintegration are largely a mystery also. . . ."

WHY
PEOPLE
REMARRY

2

If it is a myth that most people marry because they are "in love" with one another, when mainly they are attracted to each other's appearance, it is no myth that divorces following first marriages are usually bitter. Complaints by men and women about the cruelties and vindictiveness of their former husbands and wives are universal. Men become violent and kick doors in when they come to visit their children; women make unmeetable demands. The destruction of a once-working relationship is felt by both partners and by the children who get caught in the middle when the parents they love wreak incredible havoc on each other's lives.

A woman told me that she could not believe that someone she used to love, someone who loved her, someone she used to take care of and do absolutely everything for, could suddenly turn on her and become so horrible. "Our love, if that's what it was, had developed into a wicked hate. Everything we had meant to each other suddenly was ground into nothing."

One man implored his wife to be "civilized" after their divorce, suggesting that as two mature people they could handle the breakup without resorting to accusations and dirty tricks. She agreed, and they then proceeded to have the usual troubles of his doing things behind her back, he not sending the checks every month, she writing nasty letters. Divorce American style simply isn't a "civilized" affair for the most part.

Another woman told me: "Our divorce was bitter. I had to change the locks. He threw chairs, pots, pans. He was a very angry person. But I'm not disillusioned about people being able to have a commitment to each other."

Whatever form the bitterness takes, divorce always leaves two people who have grown used to the routines and protection of marriage abruptly single again. They have to backtrack and start from the beginning. Depressed, miserable, at the lowest point in their lives, they must first survive, then learn to cope.

Between Marriages

I think of the pause between marriages as a period of stumbling blindly through a dark, boulder-strewn, humid valley which at times is frightening beyond endurance, until at last, through luck and the will not to give up, one staggers in the right direction—whether toward a new marriage or a fulfilling independent life—and there is light again. It is hard enough, under the best of circumstances, to rearrange one's life—but to have to do it in a state of shock, with continuing assaults from one's former mate, makes survival almost impossible for some. People must have an incredible resilience and strength to be able to take such psychic insult and still hold on. One certainly begins again at the bottom, rejected, defenses stripped to raw nerve, ego splintered beyond recognition, biologically alive, but psychologically a mess.

As one woman explained: "I was unhappily married and miserable, but I didn't want the divorce. I had the idea marriage is forever. I thought you just go on being miserable. I never had the nerve to speak up and say 'I want out.' My ego was totally shattered when he left. I even thought of suicide, but couldn't do it because of the two kids."

Another person still appeared agitated when he said: "I had to get out of that marriage. It was a choice between either divorce or suicide.

I just picked the wrong person. I knew it was wrong, but I ignored the warning signals."

"I was really shaken up," a woman remembered. "It was like being kicked in the teeth. I couldn't sleep. I didn't want to take sleeping pills. You see, I hadn't wanted the divorce. Now I knew that I had to get my head together, and to do that I had to get my body together, get in physical shape. I joined the Y and swam every evening with the kids. Then I was able to sleep."

Divorce leaves men and women with a terrible sense of personal failure. One is always sure it is he who is at fault, "I am so imperfect that no one can live with me." But usually it is the woman who is made to feel this, believing she is not worthy. "After my first breakup," a woman said, "I felt a failure. I thought, Anyone who can't make a marriage succeed is not any good. Lots of people admire *him*. I must be crazy."

Another woman had a similar feeling: "I had been seeing a psychiatrist for several years. I thought something must be wrong with *me*, since my husband thought he was perfectly fine. I needed someone to tell me I was okay. I was always assuming if something was wrong, it was my fault. Now I know not only *I* could have caused the problems."

Yet things gradually begin to come together, whether because of a refusal to give up, because the children can't be left, or whatever. One doesn't commit suicide, although the thought may seem attractive at times. Finding the way back to complete sanity and usefulness is a tentative process, much like a child trying to fit a jigsaw puzzle together. If one piece doesn't go into the space, one hesitantly tries something else. One usually needs more money and so one looks for a job. Money, in fact, can be the most immediate headache, both for the man who has to support two households and for the woman who probably receives less than half of what she had when she was married. In addition, if the woman has not been working in any place other than her own kitchen, finding an employer who will be able to make use of her stale and limited talents, which have been out of the job market for five, ten, or fifteen years, may be difficult. She is likely to have to take an inferior job and earn less money than she needs. In fact, if she was a liberal-arts major in college, as so many are, she probably doesn't have many marketable talents. It can be demoralizing for her to have to compete with younger women, start somewhere at the bottom and work up, and at the same time keep a home going for the children. A woman remembered: "I had to take care of my son, live in a suitable place for him to grow up, try to find a job after not working for ten years. I was using up my money and not finding a job, and it was frightening."

Women usually keep the apartment or house for the sake of the children, men have to find a bachelor pad, and both will discard friends who are embarrassed by the divorce and don't know what to say. She will visit the hairdresser for a new coiffure; he will buy a new suit; and slowly and separately both will begin to do things, find life interesting or amusing once more. She learns to live with loneliness, finding advantages in not having to make the bed or prepare a large dinner because she is not committed and can do what she pleases when she feels like it. They both learn what it's like to sleep alone again (though, statistically, he is more likely than she to have found someone else before he leaves) and, finally, when quite far advanced, she gives dinner parties alone and they both enjoy dating. It's not only the emotional puzzle that needs solving but the mechanical ones. A man told me that the adjustments in the first three years after his divorce had been considerable (she may not be practiced in earning money, but he's not practiced in keeping house). He said: "I had been left one daybed, one kitchen table and chair, and a set of china and wedding silverware, and it took a lot of arranging and time to refurnish my house. For more than a year I slept in the front room on the daybed until friends gave me bedroom furniture."

The Learning Surprise

Almost everyone I interviewed told me of the surprising and unexpected learning process that had occurred between divorce and remarriage. They felt they were not the same people they had been in their first marriages. There is another myth stating that people don't change. But divorce is obviously a catalyst which causes people to change themselves, some with the aid of counselors and psychiatrists, who have only recently acknowledged that people are a lot more flexible and capable of learning than they previously supposed. The period between marriages, however painful, is an extremely important time of life. It is then, when left to lick the wounds that will never fully heal, that one can look back and analyze what went wrong, do the exploring and changing that make one strong, develop the best of one's potential, understand who one really is. And often it is a time of admitting the truth, since no one else is listening, that however much one tried to keep from letting go of the marriage, it is a tremendous relief to be out of it and free.

A young man described this period of change in his life: "I was not thinking of remarriage during this time. I tried to learn more about my first marriage, what had happened, why it had gone on for so long, why I had gotten married to begin with. It led to a new self-awareness, years overdue. It made me much less fearful of marriage as an institution. Seeing myself in new ways for the first time gave me an unprecedented self-confidence. I came into close touch with my feelings, feelings that had been trained out of me. I suddenly discovered I could relate to people in new ways that were exciting and not threatening. If I read about myself in a novel, I wouldn't think it was the same person."

Another man suggested that "the whole experience of being married and then being single again gives you a greater insight into who you are. In my second marriage, I am very clear about what I want out of life."

People report making very definite efforts at rehabilitating themselves. They zero in on something positive, and dive after it. "After divorce comes a need for self-definition. You have to be creative and learn to solve problems." Whether it is learning to fix sinks or exercising to keep fit or working hard to get a job promotion, people begin to do what makes them feel good and important again. They begin to develop personalities in their own right. They become more interesting. But recuperation from such a serious trauma is never a simple process. There are steps forward, but there is also slipping backward. And there is the recognition that part of one's past, one's permanent memories, will always include a first marriage and a divorce.

What You Miss

As people make valiant efforts to learn and re-create themselves in the form of better, stronger people, there are necessarily things about marriage they miss, and the occasional though temporary doubts. One woman rather poignantly remembered her feelings: "I don't think I've ever been so lonely in my entire life. I wondered if I had done the right thing. I used to walk home from work on warm spring evenings and see young people strolling hand-in-hand. They might stop to kiss. And the hurt of my loneliness was so strong, I could almost feel the kiss on my own lips. And there were cold winter nights when I'd see women rushing out of stores carrying packages of wine and cheeses and other marvelous foods. And I had no one to enjoy dinner with, have a drink with, have some talk with. I would go home and fry my egg or hamburger and sit alone. It was ghastly."

Another woman felt the need for companionship: "I think the thing I missed most was the love of someone my own age. When I was alone I missed the feeling of being close. The closeness around dinner hour, or before going to bed."

". . . I missed having a grown-up to talk to."

". . . having someone to sleep with every night."

"I missed weekends together. All the romantic things. It wasn't just needing someone to go to the bank or mend the toilets. I could do that as well as a man. I missed the comfort, security, niceness of having someone around. I was desperate for intellectual companionship."

This need for someone to share ideas with is very common. A male executive of a large corporation told me: "When I became single, the thing I wanted most was adult dialogue and someone to share problems with. When you're alone you don't have anyone to talk to about your problems. Women may talk to other women, but men don't talk about their frustrations."

A woman explained that after her divorce there was no one to talk to in her little town. She said she felt rejected as a woman and wasn't sure she could make it on her own. This need to talk may, as I originally suggested, be what caused so many men and women to agree to be interviewed. The story needs to be repeated to make sense. No one minded telling me again and again, in great detail, why it happened and what it was like.

The Sex Problem

After the first wave of rejection and loneliness has been withstood, and the realization of how life has changed and what is missing has been absorbed, then one looks outward again. There is a need for sexual experimentation and of ego-building through sex, because sex is usually one of the first things to weaken as the marriage begins to go. First, it is no longer as good; then it's not the same; then there isn't any. Much learning has to begin again through this route.

In a long letter a man from Massachusetts recalled the subtle steps with which he conquered his doubts about himself and came out ready to carry on in whatever new life he might find: "My divorce, now four years behind me, was an earthshaking event. I was sure that I would be ostracized and fired by my boss and that I would forever be severed from my two children . . . neither of which happened. In fact, people have been the very soul of acceptance and understanding and support. The support I received from my counseling was vital in my retaining a sense of balance and security in the time immediately after the divorce. I launched into a period of experimentation with women that was wholly novel for me, and was, in retrospect, a very mixed business. Remarriage was in my head immediately and uncritically; it was just a matter of finding the right woman, I figured. I discovered, as I began to date some of the very handsome women available around town, that full sexual relationships were not only possible but actively encouraged and desired by my women friends. It was a pretty scary venture at first. I was full of fears: I'd catch VD, I'd be reported, arrested and crucified (or something) by the irate Christians or Republicans or somebody responsible. I made some rather bad moves, propositioning women who were angered and offended. But I see their distress was as much theirs as mine. Not that I was all that active. For the most part I dated 'monogamously' in series. The net result was that I did learn a great deal about myself, in large part coming to some elementary but brand-new insights about my own value and attractiveness, learning that I was neither a beast nor a great saint, but desirably human, which is a fine thing to learn."

When it comes to experimenting and learning, women naturally feel more vulnerable than men do. It seems to be almost a traditional sport to try to take advantage of the fact that the majority of divorced women, for whom the opportunity for regular sex has been removed, are likely to be sexually frustrated and agreeable to an offer from any man who cares to make the attempt. At least this is the way men seem to see it. In the past women may have rejected sex at this time because it would have been classified as either premarital or extramarital sex in which "nice" women didn't indulge. But the truth is that divorced women and men find the sexual adjustment difficult to make, that both need regular sex, and that both expect to have sex between marriages. However, women want sex on their own terms and do not appreciate the frantic attempts men make to provide it for them. A woman from a small town in the Midwest said the minute she separated from her husband, scores of men suddenly appeared to tell her of their sexual problems. Another woman told me how relieved she felt to be out of a bad marriage but how she nevertheless missed its protection. She said that people made offensive passes at her, people whose help she needed, such as her garage mechanic.

One woman described what happened with annoyance still in her voice: "When I was married they treated me like a person. When I became unmarried, they treated me like a pawn to be pushed around and manipulated. They all wanted to play games. Most of them were married and wanted to tell me how much their wives didn't understand them."

"Dating required a tremendous amount of adjustment," a woman explained. "Men think divorced people have been around and will go to bed with anyone. It was amazing the way husbands of my girl friends came over for coffee in the morning, and before I knew it they were trying to get me into bed. I'd think, Oh, isn't it nice of him to drop over, but he was just after some easy sex." She went on to describe her evolution from needing sex to being able to handle it: "During the first year after my divorce, I had sex again. I learned lots more than I ever knew about sex and men and myself. It made me feel more sure of myself. I knew there wasn't anything wrong with me, as my former husband had made me feel . . . so inadequate. He had said, 'You know, you're not sexy and your breasts are too small.' Now there was a renewal of my ego. I found I could be attractive to men and I could enjoy sex. Then, when I knew this, I was able to turn around and say 'No' to men. Turn the offers down."

The need to repair the ego through sex is not unusual. Another woman told me: "After my divorce I had an affair right away. I had to prove to myself that I was an attractive person, to prove I wasn't what he said I was."

Having an affair, or several, and being desired immediately by someone is one of the fastest, surest ways men and women find of restoring some of their self-esteem. Merely to be desired again, to be wanted, admired, perhaps even to have the illusion of being loved for a couple of hours, can begin the job of making one feel human after the insults and degradation of a nasty breakup. Everyone I talked to had some kind of sexual experience fairly soon after divorce, but it wasn't always so easy.

"There was no problem finding dates—once I moved from a small town to New York City. There were any number of unhappily married men and men between marriages who would take me out. I enjoyed spending a few hours in the adult world, but I didn't want to go to bed with everybody, and I always felt guilty when they spent a lot of money on me and I didn't go to bed with them."

Logistics are often difficult when there are children present. One woman said: "I dated, I had sexual needs, but there were the children. Every encounter had to be planned." Another woman told me about spending the night with her boy friend, who would have to wake before the children did, dress, leave by the back door, go around to the front door, ring the bell, and make a big fuss about arriving. Until they were married, they did not want the children to know they were living together.

Declaration of Independence

As the physical and mental pieces come together and fit into place —handling a job, dating and a sex life, managing the house, the money, and the children—most people draw new and exciting strength from a sense of increasing independence. After being lifelong dependents, first of their parents and then of their husbands, women especially revel in the fact that at last, if belatedly, they have become whole and self-sustaining. "I felt so independent. I found I could pay my bills, put out my garbage, and feed my family," one woman told me proudly.

Another had a similar experience: "When my first husband left, at first my ego was so shattered, I thought no one would be interested in me. Then I enjoyed the independence of being single again. I found I could support myself, fix things, get the car taken care of, replace a light bulb. It helped my feeling of self-worth. I could handle my two kids alone and enjoy them. I got closer to them. They were an emotional outlet for giving, since I had no husband to give to."

There seems to be a universal elation at the moment each person recognizes that he or she is able to function perfectly, able to be a strong individual, especially if one has never had the necessity of testing oneself against any adversity. "I got tremendous confidence in myself," a woman who had gone back to work said. "It was almost like confronting a dragon and winning. I was able to do what I wanted to do. I went back to work and loved it. I had worked during my first marriage, but it was a constant battle. He didn't think I could be a housekeeper and work." Some people enjoy their newfound sense of individuality and importance to such an extent that they decide not to remarry. But most want to, while continuing to hold on to their personal identity.

The Search for a New Mate

When a divorced person begins to date and then to wonder about what kind of a future he wants, he often thinks about what type of new marriage partner he would like, and what are the important attributes that this person ought to have. In pinpointing what would be most crucial to them, none of those I spoke to mentioned appearance as being something he cared about, though of course attraction was given important consideration. The qualities that were given priority in the search and evaluation of the next spouse people hoped to find, or even were actively recruiting for, were:

". . . a sense of humor. It is impossible to live together and handle problems without one. It turns what could become serious rifts into manageable incidents."

". . . a person who is intelligent and doesn't need extramarital affairs."

". . . someone I could have genuine rapport with."

". . . a greater sense of responsibility, and stimulating."

". . . the most important thing is stability."

". . . I wanted maturity and integrity."

". . . in my first marriage I needed to know that other men found me attractive. The second time I more consciously evaluated things."

When people consider remarriage they are far more critical and careful, although it may be difficult to be rational at such an emotional time. They do evaluate their prospects for a good future with the person they are considering; they don't rush into a decision without totaling up the pros and cons and coming out with an acceptable score. One man pointed out the difference between the first and second time he chose a wife: "My first experience made me more cautious. I thought out remarriage carefully, because I'd had a bad experience. It forced me to examine my own feelings. I wanted to be sure that the kind of woman I became involved with would be the kind I really wanted. I didn't think about this the first time."

It was evident to me that everyone I interviewed had taken more time and given more thought to choosing a second partner, had been far more serious and deliberate. They were openly looking for responsibility, integrity, and maturity. They wanted good companions, good fathers or mothers for their children, good and loving friends for themselves, someone who could offer and give a deep closeness. On this second shopping trip in the marital marketplace, they were going beyond the packaging that had seduced them the first time, and were evaluating the contents and ingredients, information they decided was absolutely necessary to live successfully with another person.

Another of the many remarriage myths says that people always marry the same person, making the same mistake a second time because of their particular psychological needs. (I have even known people who were miserable in their first marriages and wanted a divorce, but said they might as well not bother to get one because they would probably only make the same mistake again.) I found absolutely no support for this. Many people pointed out that they had changed so much it would have been impossible for them to make the same mistake again. Not a single person I spoke to reported that he or she had married the same sort of person. Although in the past a man may have deliberately looked for more in a woman than he had before, and found someone far different, a woman probably accepted the best of what was around. Both can now look for exactly what they want, and find it. Many stressed that their partners were absolutely unlike the people they had chosen in their first marriages. "I knew I wanted someone who would have the opposite of the glaring problems that provoked the dissolution of my last marriage," a man explained. "My new wife is different in important ways. She is more sexually involved, more socially extroverted, basically a happier person, more like me." This man says: "If you find a partner who dances to your rhythm, what were mistakes before are no longer regarded as mistakes. The same personality traits or habits that were shortcomings in one marriage are assets in another."

Many people also told me that the romantic myth they had grown up on—that there is only one other person in this world who is "meant" for each of us, one Mr. Right, one Princess Charming—is complete nonsense. It may be comforting to believe that fate will eventually lead each of us to the one person in the world that we were meant to love, and it might be nice to relax and let fate do all the work, but it simply isn't true.

Ex-spouses expressed great surprise that they had met and liked a variety of people and that they could actually love two completely different types of person. I think they realized that there was not just one other person whom they could fall in love with and live with but probably thousands of others. And each time they took up a new interest, a new sport, joined a health club, moved to a new city, changed jobs, or sat next to someone on a plane, it probably expanded the pool of possibilities by thousands more. Many of us not only could live with any one or more of a thousand men or women but could also fit into and be happy with any one or more of a hundred different kinds of life. Not being extraordinarily different from each other in our basic needs for happiness, and being very flexible, we fit neatly into many different equations, many different situations. As divorced people think of what kind of life they want, they realize that, given the choice, there are many men and women and many life-styles that might fill their needs.

Why People Try Again

One does wonder, however, how so many people, after surviving the disastrous experience of an unsuccessful first marriage and hitting the depths of despondency after divorce, can pick themselves up, put themselves back together at no small cost, and decide to try again.

What makes them believe in the possibility that next time it can be different? With the bitterness of the first-marriage experience still fresh upon one, with memories of the hurt refusing to go away, with one's self-esteem painfully reconstructed, with good new feelings about the self and the future and a hard-won pride in independence, why does a man or a woman who has been through hell decide he or she wants to remarry? Why open oneself to a second failure and risk being hurt again? There are some people, of course, like Taylor, Burton, Mailer, Balanchine, and Ingmar Bergman, who remarry constantly. Five times is probably their average. For one reason or another—perhaps the instability of their lives, the capacity for being easily bored, or the drives that make it possible for them to be creative—they seem to find it impossible to live with the same person for very long. To put a sharper light on such marital fickleness, as Bertrand Russell chose to do in explaining his many marriages, "The more civilized people become, the less capable they seem of lifelong happiness with one partner." The world, it seems, is rapidly filling up with some very civilized people indeed.

It seems to be true for most people that in spite of all the devastation they have been through with one marriage, they don't hate marriage at the end of the recuperation period. They firmly say they believe in it, and they mean the traditional kind. Considering the labyrinthine complications looming in a second marriage, it is remarkable that so many people are willing to try again. Obviously, those who remarry consider marriage an essential commitment to someone they love. And there are other reasons: community pressure opposes living together for very long; divorced people want their children to have legal parents; they are lonely and find security in this symbolic gesture of permanence. People do not flounder around in the move toward remarriage. They enter second marriages the way lemmings head for the sea, with unswerving direction. Having learned and changed, they believe they can make it the second time. But they don't rush.

A man told me: "It was not marriage I was disillusioned with, but my former partner. After the initial depression, the necessary turnabout time, I wanted to remarry." Dr. Paul Bohannan of the Western Behavioral Science Institute says: "You remarry primarily because you are lonesome. You want someone to share the burdens." One of the many men I interviewed told me he always felt he wanted to be married: "I prefer living with someone else. It wasn't a fear that I couldn't survive by myself. Marriage just seems warm and nice and appropriate and correct." A minister who has been divorced said: "One of the main reasons people marry is the need for warmth, companionship, and intimacy. . . . It may look and feel like the need for legal sex . . . but sex is almost the only avenue of expression our society has offered for the communication of warmth and intimacy, especially to men. So it is a major surprise and disillusionment in many marriages to find that sex, in itself, does not produce warmth and intimacy . . . but that sex is a by-product, an end result. Warmth and intimacy come from talking, paying attention, sharing, caring, touching, spending time together."

There is a basic need for love in all people, which is probably the reason why most people marry the first time—although they may be confusing it with mere attraction. And the search for love is the reason why people marry the second time. How essential this need for love is has been demonstrated by Dr. Harry Harlow's well-known experiment with monkeys and surrogate mothers.* A cuddly terry-cloth mother and a bare-bodied welded-wire mother were both attached to eight cages containing baby monkeys. For four infants, the cloth mother was made to lactate and the wire mother was not. For the four other monkeys the situation was reversed, and they could get milk only from the wire mother. Both groups of infants were observed for a period of time and it turned out that *both* groups spent the most time with the soft, cuddly mother, even though some of the infants had to give up their milk to do so. Like all creatures, they felt the need for physical touch. If love is more important than food, it must also be more important than the less crucial basics of clothing and shelter, which would make it about the most important need we have. Many people told me they remarried because they fell in love again. A woman explained that she was desperate to remarry "because I assumed there were people somewhere that I could love and who would be good for me. I thought I had simply made a bad choice the first time. And I regretted that I hadn't left sooner, that it had taken me five years to realize that the marriage was no longer any good. During this time I had just sat back and watched everything deteriorate. I think I wasted five years of my life. I remarried because I was lonely, starved for love and sex with someone I loved, and I desperately

*Harry F. Harlow, *Learning to Love* (San Francisco: Albion Publishing Co., 1971).

wanted a father for my son. I had the feeling that life was in limbo, just a temporary thing until we replaced one divorced husband and one lost father."

The men and women I spoke to were optimistic about their new marriages. They didn't fall into remarriage the way they had tripped into marriage number one. They deliberated and sometimes they compromised. A prospective spouse for someone who has children may be able to make a good husband or wife but not a good parent, and this concern has to be included in the decision. As one woman said: "Every time I met a man I asked myself, 'Is this possible?' I wanted to remarry. I wanted a man for me. But also a father for my kids. I rejected one man I liked because he would have made a poor father."

Living Together vs. Remarriage

The problem of raising children is one of the reasons many women give for wanting to marry, rather than just living with someone. If there are children involved, they do not think that simple cohabitation can work. "I didn't like the total responsibility of two small kids and no father. I wanted very much to have someone fill the enormous gap in my life. I felt the pressure from my kids and the community to marry again." It is too awkward for children to explain new relationships to their friends when the parents live with but do not marry new partners. It's embarrassing to them and can cause great resentment.

Marriage is also considered more practical. "We lived together for a year before marriage. But we decided to marry because it's an extra commitment. When you're not married, it's always easier just to walk out if you're tired of working things out. Also, the man or woman might feel, I'm not married to you, I can't discipline your children."

There are also mundane advantages to remarriage, such as credit ratings, mortgages, charge accounts, and similar necessities which are still awarded much more easily to married people. "We lived together for a year and a half before remarrying. We didn't really care if we married. It would not have affected our friendship. But he said if we married I would have economic protection, retirement benefits, inheritance rights, and so on. So we did."

Almost all the people I interviewed tried test-living together for at least several months to verify their judgment, and to see if things would work in practice as well as theory. They also wanted to see it work on a full-time basis and not just in a dating situation. They wanted to see if they could handle the problems, do the dishes together, fill the long weekends with close companionship. But sooner or later most wanted to take the marriage step, whether they had children or not, simply because they consider marriage an extra measure of recognition. Just living together for these people was not enough. A young mother and theater critic explained: "When you marry you have to believe in your own choice, be in touch with your own responses, tell yourself that a person makes sense. Marriage stamps the union. You relax into the better parts of what a marriage can be." The legal paper is a signal of intention to the public, and gives both partners a sense of security. It is a gesture that assures both people that each intends to invest in the union. Each has, in a sense, bought legal stock in it. It may be that some people relax too much after acquiring this piece of paper. Nevertheless, it does mean that both partners will have to think twice before they walk out, because to nullify the paper requires an extraordinary amount of time and energy and recrimination.

Many times people prefer marriage because they want to reproduce the situation in which they grew up, and they feel nervous about living alone. "I didn't feel self-sufficient enough or secure," a woman told me. "I had always lived with people: first my family, then a husband. Living alone was frightening to me. But it was better than staying in a bad marriage. Women, though, are braver now. They don't feel so self-conscious."

There are, however, those who decide not to marry again, at least for a while. One woman said she could not afford remarriage because she would lose so much alimony if she changed her status. Marriage for her and her boy friend would be financially impossible. Another woman worried about remarrying because of "the tremendous amount of baggage you bring with you, not just the kids, but the scars, some raw." She thought she would marry when her children were older. Jane Spock, in her *Times* interview, said she thought about getting married again but decided not to. "What I might like to do, though, is just live with a man. Now, that's very new for me to say that. Two years ago I would have said, 'Marriage and security.' But I don't think I want the hurt of a man leaving again." Some women, of course, would like to remarry but simply can't find a suitable man, a matter made more difficult because there are not many available in her age range—her own age or slightly older—to choose from.

What's Important the Second Time

As people themselves change when they come through a divorce, the things they expect out of a marriage change as well. Remarried people have a sharp awareness of each other's needs and weaknesses. They minister to the needs and avoid the rough spots. They don't just blunder along; they pick their way more consciously and carefully. Different things are important to them in the second marriage, just as different qualities are important to them in the new spouse. "I was dominated by my former husband. In my first marriage we did things for effect. In my second marriage, warmth and friendship are more important. There's a relaxed attitude, an informal life-style. I don't want sophistication any more. Money and success are less important."

Another woman pointed out that "the second time you are more practical. Now I know marriage isn't going to be perfect." In remarriage, the expectations are more realistic. People have a greater understanding of what is possible to ask of another person and what is too much. They are no longer looking for perfection. The quality of life is far more crucial than materialistic concerns. Closeness and companionship are more important, and by this I mean true friendship. People told me they were not only *in love,* but actually *liked* their new husbands and wives. They were great friends as well as lovers, and they were not competitors.

Perhaps because the quality of one's marriage becomes more important, because one does not feel trapped, because one knows what one wants and can express it more easily, people the second time are more willing, in many cases, to break up a marriage they don't like. There are other options to consider, a greater variety of accepted life-styles to try. The changing values of society have made the traditional institution of marriage less important. Attitudes toward marriage and the family have become more fluid, more understanding. There is a single society for those who divorce and don't remarry; there are a growing number of one-parent families; there are more career women who support themselves and live the way they choose—all of which make divorce less frightening. And there are many people to talk to now—marriage counselors, singles groups, encounter groups, and consciousness-raising sessions. There are even neighborhood groups of women who just get together to talk about what they want out of life, or whether their husbands know how to satisfy them sexually. Second marriages may be better or worse than first marriages, but one thing is certain: they are quite different. There are often more difficult problems than were at first imagined, but no one I interviewed regretted having taken the step a second time. For most of them, the benefits far outweighed any problems. In retrospect, many of the couples saw their first marriages as a kind of training school, somewhat similar to the college they had left with academic degrees but little knowledge of themselves. Divorces were their diplomas. All agreed that a second marriage was the "real thing" at last. They had entered it with much clearer ideas regarding the things that really mattered, whether those things were love, friendship, understanding, or sex.

CRISSCROSSED
RELATIONSHIPS

3

A second marriage resembles a Cecil B. De Mille production with a cast of thousands. There are, of course, not thousands, but the relationships could conceivably go on and on in a never-ending chain. With two divorced people remarrying, and their former spouses remarrying others who have been divorced, while they in turn leave behind partners who also remarry, the remarriages appear capable of stretching on to infinity. Most remarrying people, of course, are involved not only with each other but with children and parents and parents-in-law and new children and ex-wives and ex-husbands in constantly crisscrossing relationships that can get pretty entangled. Nor are these people just related by law; they have complex emotional ties with each other as well. Thus, aside from the usual problems that people live with in any marriage, the occasional disagreements, the hassles with kids, there are a set of new and intricate problem areas that almost always exist in remarriage.

For example, along with the relationship between the man and the woman who remarry (which, after all, is the point of the alliance), there is the woman's relationship to her husband's children and his former wife, and her children's reactions to her new husband and his children, as well as to their own father's living elsewhere. A similar situation confronts the man who must deal with his new wife's former husband and her children and his own children's reaction to them and to her. If one or all of his children decide to live with him, things get more complicated; they are complicated even further, though perhaps in a more positive direction, when the couple have a baby of their own. This all creates a high potential for awkwardness. How, for instance, does a new husband designate his relationship to his current wife's ex-husband's new wife?

People think they know what to expect in a remarriage. They do enter into serious discussions before they remarry, and they know much more than they did the first time, but living with the obligations and demands of remarriage may be much harsher, after a while, than they imagined it would be. It's a world of heightened contrasts, of soaring positives and plunging negatives. Recently remarried men and women may suddenly find themselves inundated by strange children and relatives, new types of situations, the most disturbing annoyances, feelings of hate, shortages of money—yet all overlaid by exquisite sensations of personal happiness and love. It is not a case of the beautiful shell hiding the rottenness inside, because inside it is close and beautiful, too. Although your own life may be securely happy, there is, without doubt, a problem that bogs down the story. In the cast of characters there are the bitter ones, who resent your good fortune and your new role; and those who have supporting roles, but sometimes fight the direction; and those who are basically difficult and whom nothing can please. If ever a plot thickened, the remarriage plot does. There is nothing simple about it.

How heavy the problems or how simple and serene the solutions are depends a great deal on the age of the couple. Young people who have combinations of former wives and former husbands and children from both marriages will obviously have more problems than older couples whose children are grown up and living elsewhere. In some instances, their former marriage partners may no longer be alive; but, in any case, when the children are grown-ups, there is no reason for having much to do with ex-spouses. Very young people who have no children and who don't need to be concerned with alimony because both have careers and work can also simply disentangle their involvement when divorce comes and just forget about each other. The new family with young children will certainly have the most intense problems. One woman told me that after remarriage "I could have drowned in all the complexity. People need good will to work things out. And they don't always have it or find it."

The Ex- Syndrome

Divorce immediately makes an ex out of a once happily married person. It sets down certain obligations that ex-wives and ex-husbands have to abide by, involving money, property, and children. Carrying out these agreements, even after the remarriage of one or both of the ex-partners, can be a nasty business because of the ill-will, which nearly always carries over, however dulled by time. A woman I know (who had finally agreed to a divorce against her wishes) found her new husband a thousand times more delightful than her former one. She often said that divorcing was the best thing that ever happened to her, and she was grateful that she had been pushed into it. She was now free to live a really idyllic life; yet she admitted she still could not summon up anything better than anger and bitterness for her former husband and jealousy and hatred toward his present wife. The pain he had so carelessly inflicted had been deep, and she could never forget it. The majority of ex-husbands and ex-wives seem not to like each other, even when it's all over and when they could presumably be friends again. There is something about being an ex- that, very often, causes any interaction to become extremely difficult and exacerbates any problems that may arise.

But ex's sometimes dislike each other for no reason at all except that he or she is an ex-husband or ex-wife. Someone told me she hated her former husband just because he had remarried and seemed so happy. He had been hers, and now he was living with another woman, and that was reason enough for her. She might have been reacting to a wounded pride, or she might unconsciously have wanted him back again (she had never remarried), but her feelings remained strong simply because of the role each was playing, and not because there was much contact between them.

Very often, though, there is a great deal of contact between a remarried couple and their ex-partners. It is frequently unpleasant, and sometimes destructive and damaging to the new marriage. I hear about problems caused by ex-wives involving bitchy behavior and vindictive actions; while most of the problems caused by ex-husbands center around stinginess with money. Both ex's can be guilty of bad judgment when it comes to dealing with their children. Why people behave so badly is all tied up with what they expect when they marry, what they eventually get, and the expensive and unpleasant legal process of divorce, which, when prolonged and dramatized by lawyers who enjoy a spirited battle and want the most for *their* clients, makes everything worse and encourages hostility. Also, once one or both members of the couple decide they no longer want to be married, it seems to signal the unleashing of all the frustrations each carried silently through the marriage. There is no longer any reason not to be as drastically unreasonable as one feels like being. As the folklore says, and the psychiatrists echo, the line between love and hate is very fine. In this instance love becomes hate, with all the passion that any love ever had.

A man who has been remarried for ten years, and whose former wife has also remarried, told me in words of amazement that when he has to talk about the children by phone to his former wife, she is still difficult and angry after all these years and a second, happy marriage. He couldn't believe it. It would seem that in many instances women carry their grudges far longer than men do. Men are difficult, but they appear to drop their past much more readily, which can be a blessing for them but a calamity for their former wives, who may be counting on continued aid or support. Men are capable of just going away. They forget more easily. Start again somewhere else with someone else. Women, who probably are hurt much more deeply in divorce, do not choose to forget.

"My ex-wife is always trying to mess up my life," a remarried man told me. "She seems to pick times when things are going well. She said at the beginning that if I didn't take the kids, she'd separate them and put them in foster homes. So I had to take them."

"My ex-wife wrote me letters and called me terrible names," a man remembered sadly. "She made my life miserable. She said I spent too much money. I couldn't put a stop to it. There were constant hostile letters which were destructive to my new relationship."

"After my new marriage," a man reported, "my ex-wife began telephoning, describing the horrible things that were happening to her. In a perverse sense it helped my new marriage because my daughter left her mother and came to live with us. Having one of my kids around restored a sense of equity."

Men and their new wives are often awakened in the middle of the night by a drunken, tearful, or angry phone call from a former wife. There are demands, complaints, intrusions, angry letters. In the tug of war among the ex's, former wives are the ones who want retribution from their former husbands, while these ex-husbands usually want to be left alone. So in this area of squabbling, it is the women whose actions men recount. When it comes to money, the men are the difficult ones, and one hears more from the women who complain about men not paying their monthly checks on time, not spending enough time with the kids, and not being discreet. "When he came to call for the kids," a woman remembered with annoyance, "he had his girl friend in the car with him. He doesn't understand that I don't want to see her. And when I call him at home, I don't want to have to go through her before I can talk to him. He could at least answer his own phone." Another woman complained that her husband wanted most of their books and art objects and became abusive when she insisted on keeping some for herself. One former husband simply came into their old house and took what he wanted.

Sometimes people try to create an amicable situation, but it doesn't always work. A man said: "I'm now engaged in an effort to bring about some level of friendship and civility with my former wife. Up to now we've practiced mostly a monosyllabic mutual antipathy."

Occasionally an ex-husband or an ex-wife who really feels that divorce was best for both of them can live with whatever comes afterward. Women or men in this position are cooperative and even friendly. I know someone who has not remarried but goes out to dinner with her former husband and his new wife. It would be nice if it could always be this way, but most often it is a tense and disturbing relationship. When ex-husbands and ex-wives move far from one another, the situation is sometimes easier, except as far as the children are concerned. A man told me that he and his new wife got to the point, after being harassed by his former wife, where they thought of moving away. "My new wife wants to move to South America. If we could leave tomorrow, we would."

It seems clear that women who traditionally stay at home and raise children are more emotionally dependent on marriage than are men who have another life in the world of work. Women busy with home and children have few other resources, while a man, in addition to his job, has usually found someone else or something else even before he leaves and goes through comparatively less torment and suffering. And men seem to be brought up with less need for emotional attachment to one person and less sense of responsibility toward family and children than women feel. Apparently, the marriage is not his whole world.

The Jealousy Triangle

New marriages usually generate jealousy. New wives are jealous of former wives, and vice versa. Men are jealous of former husbands. A new wife accuses a former wife of greediness. A former wife thinks her successor is stupid, and says so. A new husband changes his drink, from a vodka and Tabasco to a vodka and tonic because his wife's former husband also used to shake the Tabasco bottle over his vodka. And he now insists on nothing but Russian vodka, scornfully dismissing the former husband's domestic brand, as though dismissing him.

There are subtle ways in which the two ex's can grate on each other's nerves. Deceptions are discovered. Threats are made: "I will take off with the children if . . ." "I'll stop sending monthly checks if . . ." There is also the unconscious tendency to make comparisons. One needs to be better than one's precedessor, to be different, to be brighter, not to disappoint. When one remarries, one is never alone with a new mate. One lives with vibrations of other people who were part of one's old life and the new partner's former life. There are constant reminders of the past spent with others—portraits, photographs, monograms, laundry marks, furniture, tastes, habits—living ghosts that go along with every remarriage.

The negative feelings that former husbands and former wives nourish, not only toward their own former partners but toward the former spouses of their new mates, are truly astounding; although at times there is plenty of justification for bitterness. A woman who has given a great deal to a marriage has sometimes been carelessly discarded, often left with young children who make it difficult for her to go out and live the profitable and busy life her old husband has found. And a man who once was gentle has been nagged into leaving as an act of desperation and survival because the marriage has stagnated. Frequently it is because the marriage was no good from the beginning. It probably was not a case of right or wrong but of a gigantic mismatch which was badly handled and caused people to be hurt. Yet the person who behaves badly often has too much ego invested in trying to prolong the marriage and finds it hard to accept divorce, even after the divorce has been decreed; and the news of remarriage can create resentment all over again. The jealousy symptoms that former partners inspire in new ones are not very pretty.

One woman told me, with color rising in her face, how she feels about her husband's former wife: "I want her out of our lives. There's nothing positive about her. I've never felt enmity toward anyone the way I do toward her. I don't think I've ever hated anyone till now. I can really understand how people kill other people. I hate what she does to our lives. She's constantly involving herself."

Another woman became angry just talking about her situation: "When I see his former wife, I feel I'd like to kill her. I feel there is a knife inside me whittling away. I wish she'd just leave us alone. Stop calling. Drop off the edge of the world. Let her go away and do her thing and leave us alone. That's the thing I want more than anything. It spoils our day when she calls. I can see my husband's stomach turning over. Since she didn't want him, you'd think she'd have as little to do with him as possible."

One woman said she had tried to commit suicide after her husband had left her for someone else. Her feelings for his new wife were anything but kind. Another woman hates her husband's former wife because the children give them problems and she blames their current behavior on the way she brought them up. A man despises his wife's former husband because he won't reply to letters and doesn't see his child or pay his share of the bills.

Any advances by a new wife to a former wife will frequently be met with a brusque rebuff or an impromptu insult. Angry ex-wives are rarely at a loss for words. A friend of mine who was going off to see her new mother-in-law who was in a hospital phoned her husband's former wife to invite her to go along; after all, the first wife had known her husband's mother far longer than she had. His ex-wife immediately said "NO!" which hit the woman like a slap in the face. "I would have different things to say to her than you would," her predecessor said and hung up.

Remarriage can easily create jealousy when a former spouse is alive and well and has obvious talents or accomplishments to his or her credit. But it can happen just as easily when the ex-wife or ex-husband is no longer living.

"His wife died, but her ghost is here," a woman said. "For example, my husband likes cheese sauce on his cauliflower because *she* did it that way. So I have to make it also. For the first six months of our marriage I had the feeling I'd married both of them. She was right here. All her pots, pans, silverware. Her things were around. All her furniture. The bed. I felt uncomfortable sleeping in their bed." To be practical, most people keep their bedroom furniture and the new spouse moving in has to sleep in the former spouse's bed. I think that, if there is any extra money, it would be a great idea to pass the good beds down to the children and buy new ones for the new marriage.

Another man told me of the time he had unwittingly made his wife jealous of his former marriage: "Our living room had twelve windows," he said. "My new wife asked a decorator to make curtains for it. When I saw the horrendous bill for a couple of thousand dollars I said about my first wife, 'Mary did it for two hundred and fifty dollars.' It just came out like a conditioned reflex. My new wife's face dropped about ten feet and there was this long silence."

The business of saying the wrong thing by accident can cause more than one moment of embarrassment. A man I know, named Arthur, was married to his first wife, Jan, for fifteen years. Then he remarried a woman named Jean, and occasionally called her Jan out of habit, especially during the first few months of their marriage. It might have been even more unsettling than it was, except that once in a while she accidentally called him Jack, her former husband's name.

Remarried women often ask their husbands how they compare with their first wives in bed, and men sometimes try to find out how they compare with previous husbands as lovers. Unfavorable comparisons can chill even the warmest of moods.

Jealousy can be understood by only one of the triangle, as with a man who resents his new wife's friendship with her ex-husband. Whenever this man comes by for the kids, he stays for an hour and makes himself a cup of coffee in what used to be his kitchen. The new husband feels as though he is the guest in what is now his own house. When they married he had moved in with his new wife and seeing her old husband in the kitchen makes him feel that *he* is the outsider. He doesn't really like living in the same house his wife had lived in with someone else, but his wife thinks he is being silly.

At times, though rarely, jealousy gives way to reason, as when a woman explained that she felt okay about her ex-husband's new wife. She herself had remarried and "this woman was never married to my present husband. I don't want anything from my former husband, so his wife can't hurt me in any way." Another woman is extremely friendly with her husband's former wife and helps her find freelance work. The former wife calls and confers about the children, cheerfully arranges the children's visiting schedule, and even thanks the new wife for taking such good care of them. And someone else was able to say that she empathized with her husband's former wife, who had moved far away and lived alone with her children. There are moments when most women probably feel some sympathy for a former wife who is after all another woman living through some of the hell and uncertainty that hits every divorced woman, regardless of the circumstances. Too often, though, these compassionate moments are cut short by some really exasperating remark or letter or phone call, and the hatred and jealousy return. Ideally, if men and women would accept the fact that marriage to one person may not last, they would also accept the fact that the partners may remarry. It would be better all around if current partners and ex-partners could, when necessary, be civilized with one another. If people did not expect marriage to be forever, if divorces were more automatic and less traumatic, then perhaps breaking up could be more painless, and a true friendship of former partners would be possible. How much people maltreat each other on the road to divorce, and how they arrive at that crossroad where each wants to choose a different direction, will determine whether they can deal with each other when necessary later on.

Ex's and the Kids

One of the most insidious ways in which formerly married men and women try to get back at each other for past inhumanities is through their children. Passing messages through children, messing up vacations and visits, and demeaning and disparaging an absent father or mother are foolproof ways of spreading an ill-will that ex-wives and ex-husbands may feel. By not accepting the demise of a past marriage, ex-spouses sometimes take pleasure in trying to get even by disturbing the happiness of a new marriage. They have found that using their children as carrier pigeons can be extremely effective, and children can also be used to report what activities are going on in the enemy camp. These parents do not stop to evaluate the damage they may be doing to their children. As far as both formerly married parents are concerned, they can't stand each other. The bad behavior of many parents toward their children is an unkindness not so much to the adults they don't like as it is to those they love the best at that moment, their children. Some parents use visiting privileges or—worse—custody fights to injure their ex-partners, although the greatest injury is often done to the children. One new wife remembered that when she was ill and could hardly get out of bed, her husband's ex-wife insisted on sending the children over. Another woman said: "His ex-wife wouldn't let him see his own daughter and son unless he did this or that. But she always relented when she needed baby-sitting. I never knew when the kids were coming. There was no schedule. They'd just appear and I didn't have food. She would send them when she wanted to go out for the evening or away for the weekend. It was an impossible situation." And another: "She tries to make me the baby-sitter, and she complains if we ever discipline the boy. The child pouts and sulks, lies and cries to get attention from his father."

A remarried man would use the occasion of picking up his two kids for their regular weekend visit to get into a discussion with his former wife about money—a discussion that quickly deteriorated into accusations and angry profanities. Furniture was sometimes thrown around, and by the time the kids left with their father, they felt depressed and miserable, unsure of who was right or why their parents fought. They rarely enjoyed the visits, no matter what plans had been made for them. The mother finally got a court order to keep her ex-husband outside of the house in his car when he called for the children.

When children living with one parent hear the other parent criticized, which is very common, or when they are told how awful their real mother or father is, it makes visiting sessions very awkward. Children may actually be made to feel guilty about loving the remarried parent, as if it were an act of unfaithfulness to the parent they live with. Parents forget that a child should grow up with a strong parental image and that their quarrels with an ex-spouse are theirs alone. Ex-spouses often try to brainwash their children into believing that their father or mother is a vile, incompetent, unloving monster because they want the children to take sides. *Their* side. For children who love their parents to have to listen to one parent tearing the other one to shreds and making accusations about which the kids know nothing—and don't want to know anything—is grossly unfair and can be damaging; yet it goes on constantly. It is as though the parent believes that if he or she can convince the child that the other parent is a horrid individual, the cause of all that has gone wrong with their lives, this unreasonable bitterness will be vindicated.

One man reported that his former wife told his kids that he did not want them or love them and that his new wife had broken up the marriage. "Of course I wanted them and loved them, and the marriage was breaking up by the time I met my present wife. But how could kids know what is true?"

Another woman told her children that her former husband was fat and a drunk. They were surprised, when they finally saw him again after a period of time, to find that he was neither. A young high school girl, who lived with her mother during the difficult years following her parents' divorce, always acted as the needed ear, hearing her father roundly criticized, and as the needed shoulder for her mother to cry on. She felt the natural sympathy that one woman feels for another who is suffering, and absorbed her mother's prejudices. When she finally spent a few days alone with her father several years later, she wrote back in surprise to her mother: "You know, I really enjoyed myself with Dad. He's really very nice." She had been forced into her mother's quarrel with her father; she herself had had no quarrel. Although her mother may have been justified and the complaints quite real, the daughter eventually came to believe that, for her, the real situation had been exaggerated. There is always another side to the story.

And a man who took his children to the zoo one day made sure that between the "Ahs" over the elephants and the "Oohs" over the giraffes, he was able to impart to his young listeners that their mother had nagged him incessantly, wasn't loving, always complained about money, never wanted to do anything, was always tired, and had been impossible to live with. He told them to try to bear the terrible situation as best they could. And another former husband really embarrassed his kids by complaining that their mother squandered the money he sent for their food and clothes. They, of course, had no way of knowing how much was spent or what things cost.

In addition to looking for allies in the war between the ex-spouses, most formerly married men and women worry about the influence the new wife or husband will have on their children, and they are often jealous of and act to prevent this influence. Most former wives, for example, are particularly worried about a new wife taking over the delicate balance of affections and giving love to kids who are not their own. To be a good parent in a blended family requires skill and patience. The new wife may feel a natural inclination to love, befriend, and advise her husband's children, who live with their mother but come to visit. Her demonstrations of affection or concern, however, can antagonize the real mother, who may feel the new wife is trying to usurp her role or even monopolize the children's affections. A new wife smiled wanly as she recounted how, when she tried to offer occasional affection and advice to her husband's children, their mother would call and remind her, "Leave them alone. You are not their mother." The ex-spouses fear that their children may find the new wife or new husband more attractive or more fun or more generous. One wife received a large box of toys from her ex-husband for their children the first Christmas that they were apart. She opened it, appraised the toys, and shipped them back to the store. They were expensive, more expensive than anything she could give the children, so the children would have nothing from their father. Such parents are afraid that their children will be won over and prefer the "other," wealthier family.

Fathers sometimes cause difficulties by trying to force ex-wives to keep the children living nearby. Many fathers enjoy their weekly visits and miss seeing their children, but when the mother cannot get a good job in her hometown, it can be unfair to her. Stipulations that a child cannot be moved out of the state may create hardship on a woman who is trying to find a new life for herself, but of course they protect the father's interests. Longer holidays and summer vacations with Dad might be a satisfactory compromise.

If the father or mother does not visit the child regularly or does not provide a good atmosphere for the visit, many parents feel it would be far better for the child if he or she didn't come at all. The disruptive parent ought to be allowed to fade out of the immediate picture and return to the child's life at a less chaotic time.

I know one father who does not relate very well to children. He saw his child only twice in the seven years after his divorce. His former wife, who had remarried, said she thought it would be better if he didn't show up at all, since his visits were so sporadic and infrequent. Under these circumstances, the child had to go through the pain of separation after both visits. When this father took the advice, which conveniently lessened his guilt and let him off the hook, the child was able to forget him and develop a strong attachment to his stepfather.

Protecting children—even if it means breaking the letter of the agreement by avoiding frequently unpleasant, though legally allowed visits—is important. The most civilized and perhaps most difficult thing for a parent who keeps the children to do is to try to build up the absent father or mother so that the child can continue to love this parent until he or she is old enough to make the necessary judgments alone and uncoerced. The child may understand that you don't like the other parent for this or that reason; but it should be made clear that this is only your opinion and that he will later have to figure out his own relationship to this other parent. It is cruel to play the game of pulling strings and making helpless marionettes out of your own children. No matter how bitter one is or how right one is in being bitter, and no matter how bold the provocation, one must always remember that it is not the children's battle.

Friends and Others

Part of the human network confronting newly remarried people, in addition to ex-spouses and children, is the host of friends and mothers- and fathers-in-law who populate the background. It is extremely difficult for friends to remain equally friendly with the divorced spouses, and they usually drift gradually, if not immediately, to one side or the other. They sometimes don't mean to take sides, but can often be very sympathetic to one or the other's problems. If the man has made friends through business or sports, these are certain to remain his friends; and friends that a woman might have in the neighborhood or at school or through clubs or sports will probably remain her friends. One man told me that his friends definitely took sides and that he lost some. Some friends, he pointed out, got deeply upset by his divorce and remarriage because it raised questions about their own marriages. The reaction of friends can often be a disappointing experience. A woman reported that after her divorce, when her former husband remarried, their old friends entertained her husband because he and his new wife "were a new thing. I was the odd woman. I wasn't needed. I wasn't invited to dinners. I had to find new friends."

Parents and parents-in-law can be problem-producing to some degree. Very often a mother- or father-in-law will like the second wife or husband better than the first, and remarriage can be a pleasant event for these older people. But sometimes, if they liked the first spouse, the in-laws don't react well. One ex-wife's father phoned the new wife continually for a while and called her bad names.

One former husband resents it if his first wife has any contact with his mother, despite the fact that the two of them corresponded regularly during the entire marriage. She was the one, not her husband, who wrote faithfully every week. Their divorce meant to him that she could no longer even write the woman of whom she had grown so fond —a divorce by association. The former husband didn't want his mother showing affection for someone he no longer liked, but at the bottom of it all was his fear that she would leave his former wife her money, or some of it.

Some parents get upset when their children divorce, as though it were a personal affront to them. "Look what you're doing to me," one mother told her daughter. But such people usually come around and accept the divorce and a new marriage, although they accept it in varying degrees. One woman told me that her new husband's first wife's parents (in other words, one set of the children's original grandparents) visit and stay with them. But it is a mixed blessing. They always ignore her children, she says, "and that infuriates me. It hurts my kids. They don't send them Christmas presents, only their own grandchildren, and I think that's rotten, with all the kids living together with us. When the girls graduated from high school, they sent his daughter a set of luggage, and my daughter only a photo album. My husband thinks it's rotten too, but my girl has learned to handle it."

There are times when, during the period after divorce, a man or woman's parents will move into the house and take over. Often, they don't want to give up this position when their daughter or son remarries and they are no longer needed, but, in most cases, their interference, if it exists at all, is distant or short-lived and they do not remain a major problem in remarriage.

The Money Muddle

One of the major problems that remarried people face is the demon dollar. The lack of enough money, or the demand for more of it, has led to great bitterness between former husbands and former wives. Besides regular visiting rights with children, it is the one thing that continues to tie ex-spouses together, when they would probably rather be able to forget each other and begin new lives. It is the one thing, besides the children, that keeps the memory of the past clouding over the bright new remarriage. This attachment cannot really be terminated until the dependent spouse (usually the woman) has remarried or the children have grown up and left home.

While the children are still dependents, people in new marriages are forced into doing business with their former partners. Even if they start a new postdivorce relationship on good terms, thinking that all will work out, the years of paying alimony and child support, the years of the wife's needing and asking for more money and often not getting it, can push the relationship to unbearable limits. Inevitably, the economic strain produces psychological strain, and many men, quite unjustifiably, feel that they are being taken advantage of. A remarried father may love his children, yet the drain they place on his finances often causes him to resent them. His first wife, regardless of what she receives, is not likely to consider the sum adequate. With expenses escalating as children grow older, it probably is not enough or even half enough. Although the new wife was prepared to cope with a budget deficit month after month, she too can become increasingly exasperated by the persistent money squeeze. One woman said: "I wanted to marry him, not him plus all his encumbrances. I wish his other family would just go away and leave us alone." A man said: "It seems as though I've been bled dry by these obligations all my life. Will it never end?"

The years when a remarried man is providing support for his first family are usually difficult ones for his second marriage, and often both the new and the old families are obliged to downgrade their standard of living. Such a prospect might be expected to discourage remarriage—but it doesn't. People usually enter second marriages prepared to make sacrifices and even willing to dip into savings. The second marriage may be possible only if the new wife works and contributes part or all of her income to support her husband's former wife and his children.

The remarriage may be flying high on an excess of love, but when it comes to money, things can be strained. One man moaned about his money problems: "I'm paying three-quarters of my salary in alimony and child care [the price of the divorce], and, while my life remains interesting, in many areas I'm living on a poverty level. Federal taxes have not yet embodied the idea that child support can be a huge expense that ought to be deductible, no matter what proportion of the total support I pay." Another man told me that the drain on his income was enormous: "One-third goes to the government, one-third to my ex-wife for child support, and I'm left with one-third for me and my new family."

A stepfather told me that his wife's ex-husband doesn't send support payments regularly, and had tried to get him to adopt the kids to avoid having to send any more money. A woman in charge of household accounts said that having to send money to her husband's former wife every month makes her angry: "I knew we'd have to do it. But it took a while for the reality to hit me. It's one of the things I have to live with. We have to pay out six hundred dollars a month."

When her husband doesn't send the monthly child-support checks, one ex-wife just calls him on the phone, "and we fight. I feel really angry that my former husband can cop out. It arouses all the old feelings of hurt and anger over his rejection of the kids." Another woman complained that the bills from schools, orthodontists, and camps that were sent to her former husband were never paid, and when they finally were sent to her, she had no choice but to pay them herself.

Lucile Duberman, a sociologist at Rutgers University, surveyed one hundred families living in Cleveland, Ohio, for a study on remarriage.* Dr. Duberman found that of the men who had stepchildren under twenty-one, 69 per cent paid all their stepchildren's expenses; 19 per cent paid part of the costs, and 12 per cent paid none. These figures would seem to indicate that 69 per cent of these children's *real*

*Lucile Duberman, *The Reconstituted Family: A Study of Remarried Couples and Their Children* (Chicago: Nelson-Hall, 1975).

fathers were not paying child support at all and that only 19 per cent were paying some of it. Twelve per cent of the real fathers may have been paying all their children's expenses or, more likely, the mother either had money of her own or worked to pay her share of her own children's expenses. Fathers are notorious for disappearing and paying nothing at all, for sending checks so irregularly that they never contribute their share of the support, and for balking if there is an extra expense, such as a new ten-speed bike or a new set of clothes. A woman charges her former husband for the postage stamps she buys to send him communications. There is a great deal of pettiness on both sides which makes financial details a continuous irritation. Lack of enough money has deeper effects on people than mere irritation. A recent study, done for the National Institute of Mental Health, found that depression among women is rising rapidly in the United States. The unhappiest are those with a low income and young children, particularly women who are separated or divorced. When the average family income sinks from $10,000 to $4000, a group of middle-class women, says the report, often become the country's "nouveau poor."

When the standard of living drops suddenly, it can be quite a shock, no matter how well prepared you may be. A remarried woman told me that she helps out by using some of her own personal savings and by not buying things she wants. "My new husband and I have some arguments over money. I worry that we won't have enough at the end of the month for his child support and our taxes. We never save." She said that money is the thing she worries about more than anything else, and life for her is now very different: "We don't entertain. We invite people for a pot of soup and French bread. We don't buy clothes. We don't travel as much. It's a source of tension every once in a while."

It is quite common for a wife to help support her husband's former wife. She may complain, but usually accepts the fact that this must be her contribution to the new marriage. It's not the working that she resents, since many new wives want to work anyway; it's just that she would like to be able to save or enjoy more of the money she earns. However, there is often no alternative. A woman complained: "We couldn't get by if I didn't work. It bothers me when we want to make a trip and can't afford it. Paying alimony and child support has become one of those expenses like heat and electricity. We've always lived with it. We accept it; otherwise we would become bitter and all wrapped up."

"If I didn't work," said another remarried woman, "we couldn't manage. My husband never could have remarried. He felt so guilty about wanting to divorce that he bought his way out of the marriage. So we have more than average to pay out every month. It's too much."

In some situations a family may both send out support for some children and receive it for others. A woman whose new husband supports his own children said she might resent this if not for the fact that her own former husband is sending support to her for their kids. But her ex-husband doesn't always send the check, and they never know what their income will be every month, which often leads to stress over money. Remarriage to women who would prefer to stay home and raise children is often impossible unless the man becomes a divorce delinquent.

Having known a number of men who send child-support checks sporadically or not at all, I can't help wondering what makes them think they are responsible for less than half, or none, of the support of their children. Do they really believe that because the woman bears the child it is more than half hers, or all hers? Probably not, but men who don't want to pay support are in an advantageous position, and they know it. Few women could bring themselves to desert their children, although it is true that more women are now giving fathers legal custody after divorce. But men who are not emotionally close to their children somehow manage to dispose of any guilt feelings that they have about abandoning them. Though having a set of double duties may be difficult, the responsibility they share for the kids is real and cannot be handed back. It is an irrevocable obligation which no divorce court should have to tell them about.

One way of instilling an equal sense of responsibility is for each married couple to think long and seriously before having children, to be certain there will be enough money to care for them and that this money will always be made available, no matter what happens. Because there are so many divorces now, any couple contemplating parenthood might be advised to enter into a contract ahead of time. Second, a couple should agree to share the responsibility of contraception, making sure that only the most effective methods are used—pill, sterilization, or IUD—to avoid accidents, which can sometimes instigate divorce. (Between 1966 and 1970, the National Fertility Study estimated that more than 2.5 million births occurred that were probably unwanted, or 15 per cent of all the children born during that period. A really sobering statistic.) Once children are born, however, both parents, the man as much as the woman, have no choice but to undertake their cost and care.

Not long ago, in a review of the latest Peter Benchley book, I was struck by this sentence: "No longer burdened by his former wife and two children—What is the word for former children?—David is ready for anything." Former children? There is no such thing as "former children." They are and always will be the children of both parents, regardless of whom they live with or where they are.

To ease the money crunch, remarried women who have their own funds often pay for their own expenses, such as clothes, trips, and luxuries. But many women don't have a sufficient income and the question of who pays for what in the new marriage can be touchy, particularly if her expenses include her children from a previous marriage and when their own father doesn't contribute. One woman remarked that whenever her son needed something which happened to cost a lot, her new husband said he couldn't have it, although his own children had been able to have such things when they were growing up. This irks her, because she feels that to assuage the guilt he feels toward them, he is overly generous in his agreement with his former wife and with his own children. Another woman told me that she resents her husband's sending a monthly alimony check to his former wife, who works and doesn't need it. At the same time, however, this woman also feels that perhaps his ex-wife deserves it because she is raising his children and ought—like a baby-sitter or governess —be reimbursed for her time. One woman's new husband expects her to pay for her son's college education, and she agrees that she should, since it is her son, and therefore her expense. The boy's real father won't contribute beyond an inadequate monthly support check, and so it has become her job to earn the money.

Constant friction over money, which exists in different degrees in different remarriages, can be like static in the hi-fi system—pretty nerve-racking, but one doesn't have to listen all the time. While the children are under twenty-one, money problems are pretty continuous. When children are part of a remarriage, there are always more expenses than one can imagine there will be, so remarrying couples ought to be prepared for the worst and decide in advance whether they can handle it, and how. Children always need more than one realizes, prices always rise, and there are always unexpected emergencies. Most people I interviewed said that money problems were much more tension-producing and expensive than they had thought they would be, but not one couple told me that they would not have married, even if they'd known at the beginning what they now know. They would have done exactly what they did, although some people thought they might have prepared for it in other, better ways.

Why do people let themselves become involved in a marriage that is far more complex and problem-ridden than their first marriages were? There are some consoling factors in the economics of remarriage. Former wives are now expected to work to help support their families, and if they remarry, alimony need no longer be paid. Children do eventually become twenty-one and more or less independent. When one remarries in mid-career, there is often property or a savings account to help ease the way in emergencies. And no matter what the difficulties, the second love is important enough to motivate men and women to face any problem, so long as they can make it together. They want the marriage more than they want the money. It's that simple.

Legal Considerations

Remarriage is so new as an established way of life that the legal ramifications are only just beginning to be explored. By the time a remarriage takes place, alimony, child support, and the division of property have already been set with regard to the former marriage; but the present marriage may raise new legal complications. In the past, remarrying men and women of wealth had occasionally demanded prenuptial contracts to safeguard their money against new husbands or wives who might turn out to be fortune hunters. Today, with more remarriages than ever in history, the legal as well as financial needs of these newly formed couples are undergoing serious evaluation. With so many crisscrossed relationships—his and her money, his and her former spouse, his and her children—people should consider what they want to happen to their estates and their legal responsibilities and reach an understanding before they take the step of remarriage. One of the new investigators in family law, Lenore J. Weitzman, an assistant professor of sociology at the University of California in Davis, observed in a paper* that "The marriage contract is unlike most contracts: its provisions are unwritten, its penalties are unspecified, and the terms of the contract are typically unknown to the contracting parties." She says that, legally, a traditional marriage contract assumes that all marriages are first marriages by saying "until death do us part." What about until divorce do us part?

People entering second marriages, says Dr. Weitzman, have different concerns which need to be recognized by the legal system, because they bring responsibilities and obligations with them. In a letter to me she wrote: "People entering second marriages would be wise to protect the obligations they wish to acknowledge to previous spouses and children of previous marriages. For example, it may be important that the second spouse agree to the first wife's retention of rights to health-insurance coverage, pension plans, life insurance, and the children of the first marriage's right to tuition for their college education, medical coverage, etc." And in the *California Law Review* article she pointed out that a "surviving wife automatically inherits a fixed share of his or her mate's estate, but there is no recognition that a former spouse may have played a greater role in building the estate and should therefore be given a larger interest in it. Finally, except by antenuptial or postnuptial agreement, or disinheritance in a will, it is impossible for those who have remarried late in life to prevent a spouse of short duration from inheriting a fixed share of their estate." Since more divorces involve children under eighteen, their inheritance rights have to be spelled out, especially if a parent wishes to leave money or property to a stepchild.

One friend of mine who had been married for thirteen years was sued for divorce because her husband had found someone else who, at that point in his life, was more interesting. My friend was concerned that, although she had received an adequate settlement and modest alimony and child support, her successor could receive all her former husband's life insurance as well as his assets if he died at any point after his remarriage. She had worked at a job for thirteen years to help support her husband and build up his estate, but he had retained most

*Lenore J. Weitzman, "Legal Regulation of Marriage: Tradition and Change," in *California Law Review,* Vol. 62, No. 4, July–September 1974.

of it in his name. She also worried that their children would not be mentioned in his new will. Had she or her lawyer been smarter, provisions to avoid these situations could have been made in an agreement at the time of the divorce. When her former husband decided that he could not afford to pay for their children's college education, she had no way of forcing him to do so, since the children were by then over eighteen and were no longer considered minors.

Life and accident insurance, medical coverage, retirement benefits, pension rights, shared investment in a career, and property rights should all be considered at the time of divorce, but if provisions have not been made, each person entering into remarriage should clearly understand who is to receive certain benefits and an agreement to that effect should be signed. Sometimes a husband may put his house or other assets in the name of his wife to prevent a former wife from claiming it if something happens to him. However, a property settlement signed by a former wife at the time of divorce and a marriage agreement signed by the new wife should avoid most problems, despite differing state laws.

The New Etiquette of Remarriage

Remarriage in the past has traditionally been treated as a private event, not a social one—probably because of the awkwardness or embarrassment involved in the loss of former partners by death or divorce. For that reason, and because comparatively few people remarried, there is no detailed etiquette of remarriage with rules about name-changing, wedding ceremonies, or anything else. People had to make their own rules as they went along. Books of etiquette usually devote most of their pages to first marriages and the thousands of details they entail. But with so many divorces and remarriages today, there ought to be a new etiquette devised to cover the new and complicated situations that may develop. In fact, it may soon be necessary to discard the old books completely. If first marriages continue to fail in such growing numbers, they may come to be known merely as preliminary marriages, with all the ceremony reserved for second marriages.

In Emily Post's *Etiquette,* originally written in 1922 but revised by her granddaughter-in-law, Elizabeth Post, in 1969, there is some recognition that times have changed. A few paragraphs concern divorce and some bits of information have been included for the remarried. Ms. Post warns that a child should never be forced to call a stepparent Mother or Father; goes on to mention the use of the words stepmother, stepfather, stepson, and so on in introductions; says that divorcées do not announce their engagements in the newspaper but write their friends instead; and she presents a complete floor plan of where the wives, husbands, ex-wives, and ex-husbands sit when children of divorced parents marry. Ms. Post notes that weddings of divorced people are small and private and suggests that the bride wear a street-length dress, but never a white, one, and never wear a veil or orange blossoms.

As helpful as these bits of advice may be, the authors are obviously straining to impose the unyielding, wooden rules of the past on a modern situation. Considering the chaos of mixed-up families, and the frequent bitterness involved, it seems archaic to try to arrange everything neatly so that the performance can go on as a modified imitation of the first marriage.

Rigid manners and rules don't seem to go with remarriage any more than a divorce goes with "till death do us part." Aside from a basic etiquette for reference, I believe that a couple ought to make his and her own rules, and for the most part, that is what people seem to be doing. The new etiquette (if that is what one can still call such freewheeling behavior) is developing out of what people find convenient rather than what may be written in any inventory of rules.

Most people seem to want to get rid of the engagement and wedding rings of past marriages and they often take them off when they are divorced. It's a declaration of freedom, and it announces to all who may be interested that he or she is no longer married. The fact that one has children doesn't seem to matter one way or the other. As for deciding what to do with an old engagement ring, I doubt if the woman and her fiancé will even bother to discuss it. She will automatically stick it under a stack of never-used handkerchiefs in a drawer, or have it made into a pin if it's valuable, or sell it, or put it in the safe for her daughter.

As far as engagements are concerned, in remarriage it is usually an informal understanding between the two people involved, and most people don't announce it formally. The wedding date may often be quite impromptu, something like "Let's get married next Saturday."

Most remarriages avoid all the problems of who is in which pew or how to get two former families together for the occasion (as happens when the children of remarried people get married themselves) by skipping all the formal trappings. They marry in a courthouse or a friend's home, and usually ask their own children and a few best friends to attend. They don't include people they don't want and who don't want to come, and they often don't include parents. A remarrying bride wears whatever she feels like wearing—something new or old, long or short, with or without a hat. A veil, orange blossoms, and a white dress—all traditional symbols of virginal purity—never even enter her thoughts.

A friend of mine who was remarrying chose a colorful Rumanian peasant dress, and another picked a long dress of creamy white with blue flying fish embroidered around the neck and wore a large hat ornamented with feathers. This was how she felt, and this was how she wanted to look at her wedding. The ceremony took place at a friend's farm, where she and the man she was marrying were guests for the weekend. There was horseback riding in the morning, and the wedding took place at four in the afternoon, performed by the town justice of the peace, whom they had never met and who arrived for the ceremony in his pickup truck. My friend had no children, but the man she was marrying had two sons from his first marriage, boys of six and ten, who were eager to participate in the ceremony. The younger boy was ring-bearer and the older one served as best man, and also decided at the last minute to play a hastily learned wedding march on his clarinet. On Monday, following a quiet Sunday on the farm, the new couple was back at work in the city, and the two boys were back living with their divorced mother and going to school in the suburbs. There would be time for a week's honeymoon later in the year.

Sometimes a newly remarried couple will simply tell their friends and families about their wedding and not bother with announcements, for this kind of news travels very quickly. However, even if the couple announces the remarriage, there are always odds and ends of people from way back in the past who will not have heard, and it is very likely that, sooner or later, one of these people will surface and create an embarrassing situation by assuming his old friend Bob is still married to his first wife. He might even compound the new wife's misery by assuming that *she* is Bob's first wife, whom he hasn't seen in ages. One woman recounted how this had happened to her, how this man had started to reminisce about things they'd done together, which of course she had never even heard about. What she did then, and the few other times it happened, was to interrupt the man as soon as possible and casually say, "You must be thinking of Bob's first wife. We've only been married for four years," and give the embarrassed stranger a stunning smile. She would then obliterate the awkwardness of the stutters and pauses which followed by immediately asking a question to change the subject, "But tell me, how long have you and Bob known each other?" Situations such as these can be as different as the people involved and must be handled in a personal way. Some occasions arise, however, that involve more than just the immediate couple, and here is where some sensible rules of etiquette—or at least civilized behavior—should be observed.

Weddings of the children of remarried people can require as much diplomacy as a summit meeting. A young girl I know, about to be married for the first time, was so petrified at the thought of having the wedding in her hometown, where her divorced parents lived but never saw each other, that she decided to be married in the groom's home in a distant state and invited only her mother. Her father and his new wife had been told a week ahead of time but were asked only to a party to be held a few days afterward back home. Everyone got terribly tense at the last minute. The mother of the groom thought it was wrong. The mother of the bride was uneasy about the situation, and the father's new wife thought it absolutely unconscionable that he was not being included in the wedding. As it finally worked out, everyone was invited and came to the wedding; the formerly married parents held up beautifully and were extremely polite to each other; and the wedding was a grand success, which could well have been even grander had the daughter included both parents to begin with. But it worked. With enough space to avoid each other if they want, I think that all parents, remarried or not, should be able to meet on common and tranquil ground for a few hours to help marry their children. If things are very tense, there is no reason why a new wife should not simply decline to attend, or choose to attend and sit away from center stage—whatever will keep the peace. The event is, after all, a joyous one focusing on the couple to be married—not on the past or present bitterness of their parents. The children who are marrying should at least talk to both parents and then decide the best way to handle the situation.

I know a thrice-married man whose son by his first wife got married at a ceremony where everything went very smoothly and naturally. The father spent his time at the wedding and reception ceremonies escorting his first wife, and though his third wife was present, she simply melted into the background and talked with the first wife's second husband. There was little resentment between these four adults, as it happened, but had there been, I am sure most participants would acknowledge that the occasion was bigger than their private battles.

Funerals are another problem time when split-up families usually come together, and when divorced and remarried people may wonder how to handle the necessary arrangements. The aunt of a friend of mine had been divorced for several years when her former husband, who had remarried, suddenly died. My friend told me: "You know, it was my aunt who was really widowed, and she was not even asked to be present at the funeral!" The husband's current wife was the official widow. In another instance, a remarried man's mother died and his former wife, who had known the woman for years, should have been present, along with the man's new wife. No one had thought of asking her, however, and she probably would not have gone if she had been asked. She would have been embarrassed, but she should not have been. Days of weddings or funerals are simply not ordinary days, and it is my feeling that these should be declared times of truce in any difficult relationship between new and old wives and husbands, children and other family. I think everyone should be included and should behave civilly. There is plenty of time to resume the war afterward.

There are other, less dire problems of etiquette that need to be considered before remarriage. For example, remarrying couples often face a question of what name the woman should take. Since the woman is older the second time around, she may well have made a professional name for herself, and she may not wish to give it up on remarrying. Married women, until lately, automatically took their husband's last name, but now some have chosen to keep their maiden names. Remarried women may do this too, of course, or keep their former husband's name, especially if it has been used as a professional name. If a woman does not take her husband's name, according to Dr. Weitzman, she may have difficulty voting, getting a driver's license, or running for office, but at least one court has ruled that "a woman's name is what she says it is." Many women solve the quandary by using their professional names at work, and their new married names for social, personal, and financial purposes. In this case, a woman should inform her bank and employer of the two names she uses to avoid confusion about checks, Social Security cards, and so forth made out in one or the other name. Some invent a new name by hyphenating old and new names (such as Brown-Miller) while others—probably most—decide to forsake their old names and use their new husband's name all the time. One can also convert a former name to a middle name (as in Mary Stewart Jones) to keep both names in sight. Whichever nomenclature one chooses to distinguish oneself, however, this is one problem that ought to be decided before remarriage in order to to avoid confusion and a hurried decision later.

The matter of introductions can be thorny. Most people just introduce each other as "my husband" or "my wife" instead of the more precise but ponderous "my second husband" or "my second wife." But it is sometimes not easy for the children, as Emily and Elizabeth Post indicate. It usually takes some time before a child can call a stepparent Mom or Dad. Usually, they ask for the new parent's approval long before they actually can feel at ease using the word. One woman remembered that her stepdaughter asked if she could call her Mom, but then she never did so. The stepson had the same difficulty, so the children ended up using a nickname which they had invented. I heard of one girl who was having trouble getting used to the idea that her father had remarried, and she hated to introduce this woman to her friends as her stepmother. She couldn't quite get the words out, so she just introduced her as "Mary." Though the stepmother was not altogether delighted by the incompleteness of the introduction, she wisely let it pass. She knew that it didn't matter much, and she also knew that the girl would think of a better introduction in due course. Many times people simply say "my daughter" or "my mother," leaving out the word "step," even though they may have their own daughters and their own mothers. It is obviously easier in introductions to people one is likely not to meet again or where it just doesn't matter to call a stepdaughter a daughter, and it can have a pleasant side effect of making a stepchild feel more secure if she likes her stepparent.

To face the subject honestly, neither parents or children nor sociologists care much for the terms we use to designate relationships in remarriage. Many people, including Margaret Mead and Dr. Paul Bohannan, both anthropologists, have called for new terms for the new relationships—eliminating stepfather, stepmother, stepdaughter, stepson—but they do not offer many substitutes. Bohannan believes a stepparent should be called an "additional parent," which he is in the case of divorce, and not a stepparent, which really means a replacement parent, as would be the case in widowhood. Children seem to find it embarrassing to introduce someone as a stepfather or stepmother and try to get around it in other ways, such as using a first name or not using any designation at all. (Sometimes this makes for funny situations in which the child can only talk to a stepparent if the person happens to be looking right at him and doesn't need to be called by any name.) They prefer to think in terms of "new" and "old" or "real," referring to their "old" and "real" daddy or to their "new" daddy. What else is there? "First" and "second"? It might be easier to say, "This is my first father," or "Meet my second father." This eliminates the awkward use of *"step,"* which has the connotation of wicked or implies an orphan or cast-off waif without parents. Another possibility is to do what the French do. Their word for stepmother, for example, is *belle-mère,* which means, literally, beautiful mother and is also used to mean mother-in-law. That doesn't translate into English with the same utility but it's a pleasant idea. Perhaps one could just borrow half the French word and say, "belle-mother" and "beau-father." We use many other French phrases like R.S.V.P. and rendezvous, so why not this one? Short of adopting a nonsense prefix, which would no doubt work once everyone get used to it, this French connotation might serve just as well as anything. Or one could say alpha and beta for first and second mother. This has a nice futuristic tone to it. "Meet my alpha-mother," and "This is my beta-mother." Sisters and brothers could be delta-sister and delta-brother instead of step. Anything instead of step! I suggest that people use alternatives to step so that it passes out of usage; whatever most people decide to substitute will then become common usage and be accepted.

Step is not the only name stepchildren have problems with. Children whose mothers remarry and are then known by a new name often want to change their own last name to conform. "My boy often calls himself by his new Dad's name. He wants to identify with him, the person he lives with." One boy in a new family changed his last name to his new father's name but began to feel guilty about doing that to his real father and eventually changed it back.

Another boy, whose mother had remarried when he was nine years old, decided on his own that he didn't want to be called one name while everyone else in his new family had a different last name. So he simply used Jones, his mother's new last name, for himself, though it was not his legal name. He went to school using his adopted name, took out a Social Security card in the new name and was known by all his friends under the new name. When he was about fifteen, his stepfather and mother decided to take him to Europe. When he applied for a passport he had to produce his birth certificate, which had Smith, his legal name, on it. He was in a quandary. Which name should he use? His legal name or the name he had gone by for the past seven years. Who was he? Was he a Jones or a Smith? Which father should he belong to? He knew if he changed his name back to his legal name, none of his hometown friends would know him. Should his stepfather adopt him to make the adopted name legal? He decided to let the passport office figure it out. When his passport came back, the authorities had given him a combination of both identities: his first and middle names were from his birth certificate, and his last name was the name he had been using. He found it a strange combination, because he felt the middle name didn't really go with his adopted last name. His mother phoned the passport office to ask if the name could be changed again and they said no, he would have to use the name he was known by; if he wanted to use his original name, he would have to have his "known as" name changed legally, since it had become his legal name. He had become mired in technicality.

Another way in which etiquette or civilized behavior can be useful to avoid conflict is the question of how one treats a former wife or former husband who lives in the same town. To make friends, acquaintances, and local shopkeepers more comfortable, it is always best to try to be pleasant in public, even when friendship is not possible. Manners for the remarried and their children are more a matter of what is natural and kind, of what tolerance and understanding dictate, than a superficial attempt to keep things neat and orderly for the sake of appearance. Never before has the institution of marriage been so informal, so human, and so personal. The etiquette of first marriage as well as remarriage involves a living, changing set of ideas which, with good judgment, can be individually designed to suit the couple. Etiquette has become a made-to-order concept instead of a strict set of rules to which everyone—regardless of situation—must mindlessly conform.

A New Literature

A young girl baby-sitting for a family of stepbrothers and sisters refashioned her bedtime stories to something that more closely fit the experience of her changes. In telling the story of the three bears, she began: "Once upon a time there were three bears. There was the Papa bear, the Mama bear, and there was the little bear from an earlier marriage."

It is true that adults have begun to write books, including some novels, about the crisis of divorce, and a few of these authors touch on remarriage. But the subject has yet to be reflected in the stories for children, in which they learn about Dick and Jane and Spot, stories that explore the basic possibilities of family life. *Hansel and Gretel* is no more apropos these days than *Cinderella.* These are fairy tales that have been around so long that we feel charmed to hear them over and over again, but there is nothing charming about their concepts. Stepmothers are not usually wicked, after all, any more than princes are likely to fall hopelessly in love with us.

What we need is a new children's literature, which will deal with the real world that children are increasingly likely to encounter. This world includes stepparents and stepbrothers and sisters. It includes changing houses and schools and finding new friends and having double sets of many things, and being able to love two mothers and a second father and a new fully grown brother, or enjoy a single-parent family without both mother and father present.

One little boy whose parents were divorced and who lived with his unremarried mother found the stories in schoolbooks and on television almost unbearable because they all spoke about the conventional family of a mother, a father, and the kids. They particularly talked about a father, and this little boy didn't have a father. At least some of the time he should have been able to identify with some of what he was reading and seeing on television.

LIVING
WITH
CHILDREN

Since more than a million children a year belong to parents who divorce and since most divorced people remarry, most children of divorce become children of remarriage. In 1964, it was estimated that as many as 20 million living Americans are stepchildren, but today the estimate might run twice as high. In 1970, 30 per cent of the schoolchildren in the country were not living with their original parents. Most of them having come from broken homes, and most of them suffered from the problems of adjusting to the disruption of divorce, of living with only one parent, and of shifting to new quarters, stepparents, and maybe new brothers and sisters. These unexpected interruptions in the secure routine of childhood (a routine that children insist is so boring, yet secretly count on and flourish in) can be very unnerving. A remarried woman who had just moved her two daughters into her new husband's home, after selling her own, told me, straining to explain exactly what she meant, that divorce and remarriage for kids is "very much like transplanting a plant. They are used to the soil where they grew up, the climate where they flourished, and suddenly they are uprooted . . . they are in a state of shock!"

However much of a shock it is for children, many studies indicate that lasting harm is rarely done. Children are extremely resilient, the marriage counselors say, and are not apt to be permanently damaged. Given the right parental help, they bounce back very nicely.

The shift in surroundings may be of critical concern for the child, but for the remarried couple, living with children can also be quite a jarring experience. There is an abundance of problems with children in a first marriage, of course, whether because of poor parenting, a bad environment, or the child's physical or psychic make-up. There is even more opportunity for complex day-to-day problems to arise in a second marriage. Children may suffer from confused loyalties and a sense of guilt. It is almost certain that a new mother or father will be resented for a time, especially if the children don't know the person well, since he or she is perceived as an intruder who is trying to take the place of one real parent rather than as someone who brings happiness to the other.

To help avoid these feelings on the part of children, a man told me he felt it is important for remarrying men to see that their children know the new parent for at least six months before marrying. Many remarrying people spring a new parent on their children too quickly, and there simply isn't enough time for the kids to get used to the idea or to think about the new parent in more personal terms. How they feel about a new mother or father is important, but he warns: "You've got to remember that when all is said and done, it's the two of you who are getting married. And I wouldn't ask my kids about what I'm doing in other areas; I'm not sure I need juvenile opinions about that subject, either."

Remarriage takes any original problems that couples have with children, magnifies them severalfold, and then adds some new ones. And it often creates a more cumbersome and less manageable family than most people choose to have these days. Most families today have fewer children than ever before in our history. The current average has dropped to 1.8, which is below the replacement level and means that couples are choosing to have no kids, or one or two, and only rarely three or more. But a remarried family, of, say, two children to each parent, will suddenly be responsible for four, and may increase to six if the couple decides to have two of their own. This becomes a very unusual family indeed, different from most others because of its size alone. A remarried woman with two children recounted how, shortly after she was remarried, her husband's three kids came to live with them, making their apartment too crowded. "I went looking for a larger place," she said, "but I felt like some kind of deviant. No one would rent to us with five kids, so we had to buy a house and completely change our life-style."

The greatest problems are probably caused when both partners in a remarriage bring their kids along with them. Dr. Duberman, the Rutgers sociologist, found that more than half the fathers in her Cleveland study had children from a former marriage living with them and it seems to be increasingly true that fathers are taking custody of children. This means that some families are going to be a mixture of brothers and sisters, stepbrothers and stepsisters, and possibly later half brothers and half sisters all living along with one real parent and one stepparent. It's like trying to add fractions with different denominators: You have to change all the denominators to a common number to be able to add them properly. Living with children while they readjust and find a common ground on which they all can meet can be quite a challenge. Perhaps one way to make stepchildren and natural children feel like a family right at the beginning is to give them all a more explicit role in the wedding ceremony itself. Perhaps they should be asked to make a simple statement at the ceremony and not be made to feel as if they are being carried along like so much excess baggage.

Sometimes in a remarriage only one parent, usually the woman, contributes children and the other does not. Deciding to take on an instant family isn't always an easy decision for a man, no matter how much he loves the woman. "I had mixed feelings about marrying someone with a young child," a remarried doctor told me. "On the one hand, I felt sort of sorry for the child and somewhat responsible. I saw the boy as an extension of my wife. It became a package deal. And on the other hand, I had the feeling I could have lived without this, having already raised two children of my own. Now I had to do it all over again with someone else's child, someone who didn't even pay enough of the expenses. There were times when I wished we could be alone."

Remarriage on a mass scale is new enough in our society so that there are no established guidelines or norms of behavior for a stepparent to follow. What we have are families of people caught in various stages of hurt, healing, and happiness, groping around for the right answers. These are volatile combinations, but if the new couple is close and very much in love, as they usually are, and deal together with each problem as it arises, the odds are that things will work out to everyone's benefit, the kids' included.

The Impact of Children on a New Marriage

It is very important to anticipate the effect that children will have on a new marriage. The younger the child is at the time of divorce and remarriage, the easier it will be for him to adapt to the new situation, and the less demanding on the new marriage he will be. A teen-ager who has a strong attachment to one parent, or to the original marriage, regardless of the conflicts, can be the most severe challenge a second marriage has to face. Trying to sustain romance with a rebellious teen-ager around (probably unmanageable under the best of circumstances) is not easy. There are emotional booby traps for everyone.

A second marriage is more vulnerable to the reality of children because in a new relationship the progeny are instantly there, unlike a first marriage when one can have several years of privacy before deciding to have children. And they are not only present but they are there with most if not all of their personalities intact. One doesn't have a baby around for several years, during which time one can grow used to its presence and help mold its habits. These children have already developed their own irrepressible needs, habits, and problems. They project their own thing, not always in the most pleasant dimensions, onto the new relationships being formed by their parents.

"Our biggest problems are those with the kids. They overwhelm any others," one woman said with a great sigh. Another shook her head: "Being a stepmother is very hard."

"It would have been a lot easier without the kids," a woman told me very honestly. "But being a stepmother made me reevaluate myself. I had thought I could handle the kids. I thought I could handle everything. I could see by their reaction that it wasn't true. Dealing with them humbled me."

Another woman held her head in her hands as she sat on the couch and said: "I've never been so tired in my life. All those children. The noise, the demands, the chatter. I can't wait till they all leave. Just two more years. But I'll make it."

Happiness in remarriage may well depend on where the children live, how old they are, and how many of them there are, but even grown children living elsewhere on their own can be a force that may buffet a new marriage. Children cause tensions. Stepparents and parents may have opposing views on how to bring them up or advise them, and will disagree over which policy to pursue. Children can accuse parents of favoritism or of being too strict, and they are experts, without any previous experience, in knowing how to play one adult against the other. Even the most agreeable, blameless child can inadvertently cause distress by resembling the divorced, absent parent or bearing that parent's name. Some parents treat their stepchildren more generously than their own children to avoid an accusation of favoritism or simply to win them over, and end up causing further tension. One woman said in dismay: "I thought my stepchildren would like me and be interested in me. They were, in fact, criticizing me, watching for mistakes, judging." Children and stepparents may feel hostility, jealousy, and competition toward each other. And children may be insulting and cruel at a time when the newly married couple wants only to think of personal happiness and a peaceful new life.

I think that as divorce and remarriage become more common and as children see families around them with switched partners, they will not be so terrified of having the ground pulled from under them when their own parents divorce. They will readjust even more quickly than they do now. They will not be the only kids on the block with two sets of parents, and they may even learn to look for the advantages in the situation. (How sublime it would be if one family had a house by the sea and the other family had a house in the mountains, or one lived in the country and the other in the city! How really convenient it could be to have four people whose brains can be picked, who can offer help when it's needed, and who can be enjoyed separately and equally.)

A remarried couple whose family included children from both his and her marriages said they loved all their children, "but the only way we can keep our sanity is to take vacations several times a year. Get away from the kids. We have to have some time by ourselves. I don't think that if we were a first family we would have to do that."

First-marriage parents might well disagree with that last remark as they look forward to their own time away from the frantic tempo imposed by children. Despite their charms, however, in a reconstituted family children from one or more sets of parents interacting with each other can create awesome pressure on a marriage.

One couple half-seriously recalled: "We often felt, let's just go away and leave all the kids. They intrude on our marriage. We just want to be by ourselves." Another woman agreed: "Kids *do* intrude on the marriage. It's become a difficult part of the fabric of our lives together. But of course we have never lived without kids."

On one level, it is true that parents regret not having a few free years alone together with which to begin their new marriage. But although they recognize the intrusion, they are willing on another level to accept it and put it into the right perspective. A man said: "It was a bit annoying; all those kids. But you understand that's the arrangement."

"Having kids made the marriage less perfect than it would have been," a woman remarked. "There are areas in which I let his kids down, and areas in which he lets my kids down. We have areas of resentment. He could have been more of a father to my daughter, for instance. He resents her because she's a slob and leaves a trail of garbage wherever she goes. She can't arrange her time. These areas of resentment exist. We'd have been better off without them. But they stay small in our lives."

I think many of the complaints about children that I heard, after I had asked some questions, might come forth just as naturally if mothers and fathers in a first marriage were asked the same questions. If children disrupt remarriage, they almost certainly also drain off the privacy of a first marriage in a similar way, except that there are usually fewer children involved and they didn't become family members the minute the wedding ceremony was over.

For instance, children are just as likely to interrupt a spontaneous sex life in a first marriage as in remarriage, although the awkwardness of their presence during the honeymoon years of a remarriage will certainly be more keenly felt. At such a joyously private time in one's life, the presence not only of one's own kids but of his or her kids, who are still strangers, perhaps hostile strangers, is certainly unnerving.

"It's hard to have sex with his kid in the next bedroom. It's very inhibiting," a woman said. "And if my child comes in to kiss me goodnight when my husband and I are in bed, he thinks it's an intrusion."

"They interrupt our privacy and our sex life. There is always someone at our door," a woman confessed. "They came close to ruining our marriage. I was afraid of his children. They are powerful personalities. A lot of energy and noise. They overwhelmed me at first."

A man remembered when his seventeen-year-old daughter, who was living with her remarried mother, began to have problems, the usual teen-age variety. But instead of suffering through them as others did, she decided that a change of scene would help, so she left her mother's family and went to live with her father's family, in which there were very young children. He complained that having his seventeen-year-old daughter suddenly living with him and his new wife took a lot of freedom away from their sex life. "We like to have sex in front of the fire at night after the little kids are asleep," he said. "It's inhibiting having her around, especially when she's living in the room next to ours. She's in the way. But we'll live with it till she goes."

I suppose it would be ideal if all remarrying couples could be alone to enjoy their newfound bliss undistracted by lost mittens and pillow fights and food dropped under the table. But for couples with children, this is just not possible. They will have to wait till the kids grow up and be satisfied with grabbing their privacy when they can. What makes it possible to deal with so many obstructions to the euphoria of a new marriage is that most remarrying people themselves have children they love. They have loyalties to the child and to their new partner, and they love both very deeply.

His Kids vs. Her Kids

Trying to select good examples of problems that remarried parents have with their own children and with their stepchildren is almost impossible. They are infinite in their variety and span the whole range of childhood behavior, but there were several general areas of difficulty that were mentioned fairly often in the interviews. Having to learn to love someone else's children, for instance, children who often resist and reject you, is not easy. Nor is it easy for the child to adapt to one or two new stepparents. Suddenly he must switch over from a single mother and father image to two different models for each role against which to measure himself. It is difficult for children to keep two fathers and two mothers separate in their minds, and this problem can result in contradictory or unpleasant behavior. Often parents will inadvertently compound the problem by telling the child to do the same thing in contradictory ways or by offering conflicting advice.

Psychiatric social worker Belle Parmet warns that "Lots of people assume when you form a new marriage you have instant love, an instant family. They think once the new family is constituted, the kids will love the new father. And he will love the new kids. And everyone will live happily ever after. But it's very complex for children. There are complicated loyalties to biological parents and rivalries with the new parent and new children in the family, and they need help working things through. It's one of the myths we have that people must love each other instantaneously or else feel guilty and withdraw.

"The problem for children is not knowing how they are supposed to feel. If they don't love the new parent, it's not acceptable. Yet this can't happen quickly. The most painful problem to watch is kids feeling they can't be loved or have loving feelings for a new parent without feeling disloyal. If they could add this new loving without being torn apart, they could weather it. If they love a stepparent, does that take anything away from the love they have for their real parent? We haven't clarified to them that there's enough love to go around. You value your unique love for your real parent," Mrs. Parmet pointed out, "but it's not disloyal to also love others. If we could help kids work this out, help them see that they are not giving anything up when they acquire a potential new loving relationship, this may be the most important thing we can give them in such a situation. Neither child nor stepparent can give instant love, though. It depends on the age of the kids, but it often takes years to weld the new family together."

When his children and her children in varying numbers and sexes become part of a new family, there is bound to be a wide variety of personality clashes and liaisons. Remarriage doesn't always include children from so many quarters; sometimes the only children living with them are hers, either because he doesn't have any or they are living with their mother and visit. These weekend brothers and sisters offer an extra dimension of complexity.

There are times, even in a first marriage, when at certain ages, brothers and sisters will become competitive with each other and then eventually grow close together and become best friends. This happens in remarriage, too, but because not all the children grew up with each other, the relationship among them is very likely to start off with jealousy and competitiveness, with kids vying for favor and measuring each against the other. Getting used to new ways and new siblings takes time, and creating an instant family is bound to make a few waves in the meantime. The worst thing to do is to try to force children to like each other. It's got to develop little by little. As one woman told me: "If you throw two kids from different families together and nothing happens, you'd better get the antennae out. All hell will break loose. They've got to behave abnormally, or it's not normal!"

In many cases stepbrothers and stepsisters get along very well and really like each other for a while. One woman told me the stepsisters in her family were close the first year and later started hating each other. In another family the two stepsisters of the same age were sometimes best friends, sometimes intensely jealous: "It changes from month to month." In another family, his children are jealous of the attention he gives his new wife's children and they resent their father marrying again. They still want him all to themselves. He still loves them but now also loves his wife's children and gives them a lot of his time.

New parents and original parents have to be prepared for the rocky moments. There are conflicts that have to be resolved, as in an original family, but in the case of remarriage, the parents have to realize that a little extra explaining is probably necessary to make children understand what the new arrangement offers and what they must do to be part of it. They must be told that their new stepbrothers and stepsisters also have problems and feelings.

In one remarriage a man with two children who live with his former wife remarried a woman who also has two children. When his children visit, the four of them do not, at the moment, get along well. One of his girls is particularly jealous of one of his wife's daughters and on one occasion managed to put her shoes in the toilet, hide her clothes, and break her hamster's cage.

In another family the husband's twelve-year-old daughter and the wife's eleven-year-old daughter were roughhousing in the living room and a favorite piece of sculpture was broken. The girls hid it behind the curtains and his daughter made her daughter lie about it. The mother realized: "They wanted to see how I would react, how my husband would react. It's his kids against mine, and his daughter works on me through my daughter to challenge my authority. She's very manipulative."

In a third instance a woman explained that her husband's children are jealous of hers "because of what we have together. I know what pleases my children, I know when they're hurt and not saying so. I never can know with my husband's kids. I can intuit with my kids. There are times when you know they want you and you put your arms around them. I didn't know this with his kids and when I'd try, they'd pull back. Later they'd take it out on my kids."

Another cause of dissension lies in the inherent differences between children from different parents. One set of children may be used to strict discipline, the other set to permissiveness; one set may be used to an outgoing, natural interaction, the other may be used to a more sedate and reserved atmosphere. In one family two stepbrothers didn't get along and had to have separate bedrooms. They were five years apart in age, but that wasn't the main problem: his boy was organized, neat, did everything the same way all the time, while her boy was sloppy. He had been a placid boy but became mean and unpleasant. "He was jealous of my husband's son and my relationship with my new husband." In another family one boy was an outgoing athlete and the other was a reader and introverted. They had to share a room and, inevitably, there was trouble. In another instance a boy used to be his mother's favorite, but in the new family he didn't hold that position any more.

Another remarried couple I spoke with each contributed a boy and a girl. The two girls were of the same age and became great friends, but it wasn't so easy for the two boys, one of whom was hyperactive and the other was a quiet child who liked his privacy. They are learning to live with each other, but slowly. Two other sets of children in a remarriage had different religious backgrounds. Her kids had been brought up in the Jewish faith and his were Unitarian. Said the mother: "So we celebrate Chanukah and Christmas, and combine both customs. His kids had to get to like chopped liver and gefüllte fish."

One remarriage brought together one set of children who loved clothes and one that didn't care about them at all. "My wife spent more money on her kids than I did. Mine were artists, not materialistic like hers. Hers drank and mine didn't. It did cause tension. But our kids got along well anyway. They just had different interests." These children realized they came from different backgrounds and had different genes, different values. They didn't make invidious comparisons. Each did what he or she wanted and everyone was tolerated. But sometimes parents themselves make the comparisons. One new husband was critical of his wife's children because he thought his own child was better behaved and smarter. But adding up the virtues of his child against the missing virtues of her children just didn't make sense. Even children born in the same family can be total opposites.

If blending the kids is handled with extreme care, and there are not other, more basic problems present which were there even before the remarriage—problems that divorce gets blamed for—as is so often the case, things should work and all the kids should end up good friends, at least admiring and respecting each other. One woman explained what seems to be generally true: "Stepbrothers and stepsisters have both good and bad relations with each other. There are jealousies, but there is love. There are probably more good relationships than bad ones."

Children vs. Stepparents

Children and their new parents often end by developing a close and affectionate relationship, but getting there can be a difficult time for both.

"My son doesn't know how to deal with my new wife. He can't figure out what his relationship should be," a man reported.

"His older daughter has not yet accepted me. But the younger children have come closer to me because they need a mother figure," a woman explained.

A fourteen-year-old boy had been close to his mother, and when she died, he transferred his dependence to his father. When his father told him he was remarrying, he was shocked and felt that he was being betrayed. After a year he was still unable to accept his new mother completely and still resists any changes she wants to make in the home. A child who has lost a mother or father through death or divorce will usually slip into the role of surrogate wife or husband to the single parent, cooking, cleaning, and spending a great deal of time with this parent as they comfort each other. Such a child is very likely going to be jealous of any adult who usurps his or her place. A man told me of his daughter's resentment: "All of a sudden there was a new woman in the house. My daughter hated the new furniture. She would ask, 'What was the matter with the way the room was?' "

With children whose parents are still living, the loyalties remain. A woman remarked that the only time she and her new husband ever fought was over children: "I had great, vivid daydreams about what it all would be like. I imagined they would like me, come and see us. But the only time his daughter ever came was when she needed money. She subconsciously rejected me, and she treated me with less interest and concern than she treated a stranger she might be introduced to. It constantly upset me. And there was nothing I could do about it. Why did she feel she had to pick her mother *or* me? Why couldn't she have had us both?"

One woman felt that her stepchildren resented her because she took better care of them than their own mother did, but surely she would have been resented just as much if she neglected them. Very often you can't win either way and must simply accept the fact that you are going to be on trial and even criticized for a long time.

I realized what the tensions can be when my husband and I left a house-sitting couple with my son, who was then fifteen. We were gone for several weeks, and during this time his attitude was one of constant surveillance to see what the new woman did wrong—in other words, different from what I did. It upset him that she did not do absolutely everything in exactly the same way and he wrote us that he thought it would have been easier had he been left alone instead of having to spend all his time looking after the people who were supposed to be looking after him. As difficult as this adjustment was, it must be far more difficult when children know the missing parent isn't coming back. Of course, knowing this may also help them adjust sooner than my son would have. But how hard it must be for the child who realizes there is no returning. No way out. No way back to the way it once was.

Knowing all this, stepparents usually expect to be infinitely tolerant and understanding, even when stepchildren treat them unfairly. They realize that kids are going through a trauma that their remarried parents have already been through. The period of adjustment for children after a divorce can be far longer than it is for remarried parents. While the remarried couple are enjoying the love and affection of another person, erasing the heartaches of the first marriage, they must give the children a chance to catch up with them. It may take a few months or years, but consistent, patient treatment will usually win out. If the new boundaries are clearly defined, and love is abundant in spite of rebuffs, most healthy children will respond when they realize what is needed of them and they become able to return the affection.

As a measure of how easily some relationships take hold and how much more slowly others are to become established, Dr. Duberman found in her small group that the stepfather was more likely to create and maintain a good relationship with his stepchild than a stepmother. She found that among stepfathers, 45 per cent said their stepchildren felt love for them and vice versa, whereas only 18 per cent of the stepmothers felt the same mutual love. It may be that the fathers were less sensitive and called any sign of affection "love," while the mothers looked for more intense feelings. Or it may be, as Dr. Duberman points out, that mothers spend more time with children than fathers do—thus increasing the opportunity for disharmony. She also noted that the age of the children made a large difference. Where the children were under thirteen, 75 per cent had an excellent relationship with their new mother. The younger the child, the less he or she remembers another life, apparently, and the easier it is to accept a new one. The older child must struggle with feelings of loyalty to absent parents, is generally more set in his habits, and is in a more independent age group anyway.

As far as the family relationship and communication are concerned, Dr. Duberman reported that 82 per cent of the families she studied had an "excellent" or "good" parent-stepchild relationship, which was far higher than she expected, and that only 18 per cent had a "poor" relationship. Dr. Duberman believes that how the parents and children in a new family get along depends quite a lot on what kind of harmonious relationship exists between the two members of the new couple.

In general, relationships must be easier to develop when the child lives with the stepparent full time. When the child is with the other parent, the relationship you are trying to improve or create is much more tenuous. A woman who wanted to be equally close to her husband's children and her own found that her husband's children didn't want a relationship. His daughter was especially close to her own mother, with whom she lived, and felt that she should spend all her time with this mother who had not remarried. She never came to see her father and his new family unless he made a specific request, which happened about once a month. The woman explained that "His daughter resented me and looked on my solicitude as pushiness. If I asked anything about her future plans, this was aggressiveness. I could not be natural or Me. I had to remain at a distance. I found it frustrating that I could not give love to my husband's child when I expected him to give so much fatherly love to my child who lived with us."

Speaking of love, a rather curious reaction can occur when children who have been brought up in a relatively undemonstrative atmosphere come to live with a stepmother who is warmer than their own mother. They can find the affectionate display of kissing and touching quite startling, and it may take a long time before they will show their own feelings. One woman I spoke with ran into a problem of this kind with her husband's children "who don't display anger or emotion. I came from a family where emotion surfaced." The children drew back from her offering of love because the style of showing these feelings and emotions was so different from what they were used to. "She is cold as ice, like her mother," this warm, friendly woman said about her stepdaughter, "but I can wait."

There are other problems besides emotional ones that make living together an uncertain venture. Messy kids and neat stepparents, neat kids and sloppy stepparents, picky-food-eating kids and gourmet stepparents, loud kids and quiet stepparents, calm kids and overactive stepparents, willing kids and new parents who have difficulty dealing with children—all of them will have trouble sharing the same house. Children whose habits are ingrained by other people are not going to be integrated easily. This is hardly the situation one would design for a newly married couple to live in. A remarried woman said: "If I had had to live with that wild son of his, the marriage never would have worked." Another woman was still upset as she recalled her new husband's daughter: "The girl was a terrible problem to me. She dressed from the flea market and slept on the floor. She kept incense burning and invited her long-haired, smelly friends home. She'd call me to be picked up in the car when least convenient and I had to get her. She'd disregard what I had set up and refuse to do anything I asked."

And at the beginning children often try to capitalize on the new situation they find themselves in by attempting to get the most from their divorced parents. A remarried man described how his son would ask his mother for money for something and then call his father and ask him for money for the same thing. He hauled in quite a large amount of loot that way. He knew his parents preferred not to talk to each other unless it was absolutely necessary and he counted on their not communicating. It was years before they caught on, but after that, one parent never gave him anything without checking with the other.

Mothers are usually more aware of domestic problems than fathers are. Even the women who work are most often the managers of the household and have to deal with the children more regularly. In a remarriage it is important for stepfathers to decide consciously what their role will be in dealing with children. The new father is faced with a child who probably is still a bit confused about his parents' divorce and not feeling very happy about life. Before the marriage the prospective father was probably introduced to the child to see if the chemistry between them flowed, and the child very probably appraised the stranger and wondered what sort of father he might make. A woman told me that she married her new husband partly because her child liked him so much. "Even if I loved him, if my child hadn't liked him, I wouldn't have married him." But after the marriage takes place, any new father must realize that at times he will be seen as nothing more than a bothersome intruder, the person who takes mother's time, the one she now gives more attention to, the stranger she covers with kisses. It's hard for the child to swallow this all at once. But if the new father is smart and willing to be patient, realizing that adjustment takes time, he can help put the child back together again. Sometimes the child may want a new father very badly and the stranger will be warmly accepted. Children who feel this need may give the new dad a lot of attention, demanding that he play with them, love them, asking to sit on his lap. They may even try to keep Daddy for themselves so Mummy doesn't get him. One ought to be generous with affection, which is relatively cheap to manufacture and so valuable to give. But a father pointed out that one has to remember the role one is filling. He said: "I never play substitute father. I never make their father look bad." And with other children in their teens, it is usually best to try to let them decide how much of a close relationship they want and treat them accordingly. A father said about his older stepson: "I was more of a friend than a father. It was man-to-man." The relationship supplied closeness and affection without being too paternal.

Whatever efforts the stepfather makes, the real mother sometimes believes that her new husband doesn't do enough for her children. One woman often told her husband: "If they were your real children, you'd take them to a football game, or you'd spend Sunday out with them, or you'd help them more with their homework."

But the stepparent relationship can be a very difficult one. As one cheerful woman put it: "He feels they're not his children, and the kids wonder who is their ruling father. They've solved it by deciding they have two fathers and two mothers, and my husband is able to act the part of one of the fathers."

Problem Children

Most children who go through the divorce period seem to come out of the experience in good shape. The interim periods, though, when things are being sorted out in their minds, can be rugged for the remarriage and for the children. Children often feel that the absent parent doesn't want them and may try to take out their insecurity and resentment on the people they live with.

Divorced parents have a pernicious habit of spoiling their children either because they feel guilty (particularly in the case of the parent who leaves) or because they want the child's affection (as in the case of the one who stays), and the natural instinct is to smooth over any feelings of anger and deprivation the child may be exhibiting. But it is to no one's advantage to corrupt children by constantly giving them their own way. It makes them impossible to live with, and it doesn't make anything right or put anything back together again. It just makes it harder for them to understand their parents and their own roles in any realistic terms. Children usually respond well to sensible, honest explanations and direction, even if you tell them they must learn to adjust to *your* life, because that's the way you want it. But one should always try to be fair with them. The best thing is to stick as closely as possible to the familiar patterns, with regular school, prompt meals, the usual weekend entertainments, visiting friends, and normal vacations. Of course, there are the bad times when the parent they live with will have to be patient or play the role of both parents, but the closer to the old procedure the parent stays, the more intact the child's world will remain, and the happier he will be.

The parent who leaves must also establish some kind of regular and secure bond with his kids and be faithful to it. Men often get tired of prearranged visits with children, become involved with other people and projects, and renege on their duties. This creates havoc in a child's mind, and he becomes sure of what he always suspected—that his father left because he doesn't want him any more.

One must remember that children are flexible, but there is no need to engulf them with your feelings and infect them with your bitterness and guilt. They have feelings of their own to deal with. Any child will miss an absent mother or father at times, but children can miss traveling parents, and go to boarding schools and camps without serious injury if they are made to feel basically secure. Healthy children have the capacity to bend with life. Their minds are supple like their bones, not stiff and brittle. Parents who suffer should do so in private as much as possible, or they will run the risk of upsetting the children more than the divorce did. In the maelstrom of emotion that divorce creates, however, it's not always easy to be rational. You don't usually stop to think about the effect you are having on others; you just react. One new wife was better able to see what was happening than her husband was: "He wanted to give them everything, anything they asked for. Guilt! And they knew it. They would ask for everything from him."

Another new wife noticed the same thing going on with her new husband and his former wife: "He feels guilty and buys too much for the kids. His ex-wife does too. Both seem to think it's a visible sign of their affection. The tone of voice he uses with his kids is overly sweet. The boy makes his father feel like a cad if he doesn't give him everything he asks for." It's bad enough to live with a spoiled child, but when this child lives with you on a part-time basis, it can be particularly exasperating because one is powerless to effect any unspoiling.

A chagrined new wife and weekend stepmother complained to me about the child's mother: "Her spoiling his kids upsets us fantastically. It intrudes on our marriage because we worry and because they behave so badly. It's frustrating. But it's a part of life we can't do anything about. She bribed the boy to go to camp by offering him a stereo set. She buys things for him any time he cries. The boy is spoiled rotten."

Many wives in a second marriage experience these feelings of annoyance at the behavior of spoiled children and frustration at being unable to change anything. It can be very difficult to convince a new husband that his children are spoiled. Former husbands tend to protect and defend their children, whatever their behavior, because it lessens their sense of blame.

Those who treat their kids like tribal chiefs are not as aware of how much damage they do—not only to the children but also to the helpless observers. Other children in the family or friends will react, often negatively, to unfair or overindulgent behavior in a guilty parent. And, as we have seen, the new spouse can suffer considerably. One man I know feels so guilty about his divorce that he gives his children extraordinary preferential treatment. Although he refuses to play tennis with his wife because she isn't good enough, he never fails to set up a game with his daughter (who plays no better than his wife) whenever she arrives for a visit. Minor as this may be, his wife finds it aggravating and visits are rarely free of tension due to the competitiveness and the hurt feelings.

I think parents who want to divorce should take the time to explain to their children the reasons, even if they may seem obvious, before the separation actually takes place. Parents with a clear conscience should not have to bribe their children into understanding and liking them. In the long run a child will respond better to honesty and to being treated like a human being rather than an extortionist to be bought off or silenced.

The feelings of guilt that men and women harbor when they leave a marriage are often relics of the time when divorce was frowned on. There is no reason for a man to assume everything is his fault, or for a woman to suppose that there is something wrong with her. Even if you know you are doing the right thing for your own happiness, you may feel guilty for doing what *you* think society thinks is wrong. In interviews guilt was mentioned more frequently than anything else as the factor that most inhibited the course of readjustment for all concerned—children, ex-spouses, and new spouses. If a divorce occurs because one or both partners are no longer happy, the children will eventually have to accept it. And they should not be bribed to accept it or showered with attention and given special treatment. At the same time that their little hands eagerly reach out for what you are proffering, they will probably be ridiculing you for giving it to them, and for allowing them to manipulate you. And everyone suffers.

When the divorcing adults in a family suddenly begin to fight and behave like madmen and monsters, sensitive children find the hysteria contagious. Spoiled children, children in hysterical surroundings, and those who think they are not wanted become angry children. They are likely to be angry and misbehave until things settle down and some atmosphere of love returns to the house. While they are testing how much they can get away with, they create many problems.

Sometimes children brought into a new marriage will, if they are still feeling resentment about the divorce, try to sabotage the relationship between the remarried couple. Some kids will make a new wife feel she is nothing more than a housekeeper, brought in to pick up their clothes and clean up after them. One new wife told me: "At times I was so distressed, I thought of driving off the road." Sometimes it's the new husband who sees his wife's children trying to get away with bad behavior. "Once her boy had a car accident; he drove into a tree. But he told his mother a different story. When I confronted my wife with the facts, she refused to believe me. Her kid had lied. And I knew he was lying. I had heard him discussing the whole incident with his friend. But I backed down. I didn't push my wife. The boy knew I knew. I had won the battle. Had I persisted, I was not sure I would have won the war."

Since a parent tends to protect his own children, the offspring sometimes refuses to obey a stepparent because he knows his own real parent will back him up. It's vital for the real parent to support the stepparent whenever possible, or the family will find itself choosing sides in a contest. And successful marriages are not contests.

Dr. Bohannan told me that food is one of the most commonly mentioned problems, a big thing in kids' lives and the one thing they tend to remember years later. In a new family, the style of cooking may be very different and children usually react to changes in food, even using it as a weapon by making chronic complaints or unfavorable comparisons. One woman told me that both her new husband's children were extraordinarily fussy eaters. The boy would eat only hot dogs and candy, while the girl ate only steak, hamburgers, cookies, and candy. "They refused everything else I set out on the table. I told my husband we'd better eliminate their whole game right away, and I told the kids the kitchen was closed after three P.M. so they could not get snacks. They were starving by dinnertime and had to eat dinner. And unless they did, there would be no dessert. For a while they refused to eat. It took a week and a half for them to decide they could eat salad without throwing up. Then everyone relaxed and we all became friends. " Another woman complained that her predecessor "runs a different house. There is no training to be neat, no table manners. The kids slouch, shovel food into their mouths, chew with their mouths open. What can I say? It's disgusting. But if I complain, when they go home to their mother she'll say it's okay."

In another instance, a son visiting his father, who had just remarried, sat down to dinner and began eating the first course, a cocktail of succulent, small shrimp, which the wife had not deveined. After munching several shrimp he held one up with contempt and said, "I'm not going to eat shrimp with the shit still in them!" He could have said nothing and not finished them, but he knew he had the power of rubbing everyone the wrong way, of being critical of his new stepmother, and he delighted in the opportunity to inflict a little irritation.

Often a child's bad behavior is a kind of game, like the one where you try to outstare the opponent. Children are sure that parents will give in and blink before they do, but when parents outstare them, outwit them at their own game, they may well become more impressed than angry and give up the battle for a while.

Part of the excuse for troublesome behavior comes from the fact that children who live with only one of their real parents will naturally idealize the absent parent, usually the father. One father even went so far as to tell his little boy: "Call me if you are unhappy. You can always come and live with me." Of course he had no intention of taking his boy, but the child didn't know it. To him, his father was a kind, generous, loving person who would give him anything he wanted and never scream, scold, or smack him. He had forgotten what his father used to be like, and built up an image of a generous, jolly Santa Claus-Daddy. So long as a father encourages this, the child is not likely to cooperate with his mother or with a stepfather who may have to discipline him at home. Increasingly often, an older child will leave the mother and move in with the father and his new family. This usually ends up by hurting the mother and contributing problems to the father's new marriage, especialy when the child finds out that fantasy fathers are not for real.

Discipline: Sparing the Kid or the Rod?

Children have to be held to certain codes of behavior or else there is anarchy. But disciplining children in remarriage is a bit harder than in a first marriage; other factors besides what the kid did or did not do enter into the situation. Not all the children are "yours," and there are often conflicting ideas about who should discipline whom. There are, once more, no hard-and-fast rules to follow, but it is important to establish some as soon as you can.

One man remembered that "When you first get married and then have children, you make the rules gradually as they grow up. But when you remarry someone with kids, their rules are different. You have to renegotiate everything. To settle disputes we decided to have family meetings every Tuesday after dinner. One kid chaired the meeting. Another took notes. My wife and I stayed out of it. The problems were aired. The children could discuss the difficulties themselves, and know exactly how another person felt." This sensible method of self-discipline will work, of course, only with older children and cooperative ones. But it's a good idea to try on kids who have made life a problem for the household.

Another man told me that the same method was used in his house. Rather than finding the problems aggravating, he actually enjoyed the whole process of finding solutions. "I loved the talks we had. They were like mind-exercises. It did everyone a lot of good."

What does one do when physical discipline is required, the children are his and not hers, and she is the one at home who must contend with the child? It's not as easy to discipline someone else's kids as to correct one's own. A woman frankly admitted that, in a moment of exasperation: "Hitting my own kids is a great relief, a way of getting rid of anger. Hitting someone else's kids seems more like child abuse, as though I am guilty of assaulting them. Their complexion is a different color, their eyes a different color, the shapes of their faces are not my shape, they are distinctly someone else's kids, guests who will always be with us."

Another woman told me she spanked her own children more than her husband's. She never felt comfortable spanking her husband's kids: "I wanted them to like me too much." But perhaps the most common situation was this one, expressed by a new mother who said: "I tried in the beginning to be a friend more than a mother, I tried not to lose my temper with his kids, to be calm, but it was very frustrating for me to act like that. Now I lump them all together and discipline them the same way."

One of the problems in the discipline is not just different forms of behavior in the kids but different theories of discipline held by the two parents. A woman complained: "I resent the fact that I'm supposed to take equal responsibility for his children of eight and ten who are not my own emotionally. It's very difficult to raise kids who have already been raised in another discipline. We disagree on how to treat them."

People have different reactions to children that don't always correspond. "My husband is permissive," a woman explained. "He talks to them and gives them a choice. Then they do what *they* want. I'm more strict. It was hard at the beginning. For example, if I needed help I'd say, 'Please do it now.' But they'd assume they had a choice, and didn't have to do it if they didn't want to. A few times I got into fights with his kids and he'd step in to protect them. I'd get angry. We agree with what's wrong with the kids, but disagree on how to treat it."

Another woman said: "My former husband was permissive, and I was the Wicked Witch of the West who clamped down. My kids, who were used to my ex-husband, didn't like my new husband, who is more like me, explosive. He raises his voice, he screams at them if they are nasty. But now they respect him."

If mothers have problems disciplining children from different backgrounds, they will almost certainly have more problems with children who just visit and are under the influence of the parent they live with.

If they are only weekend residents, one cannot expect to force a total change in habits and behavior that may conflict with what they are used to in the home where they spend most of their time. Some latitude will have to be allowed, while still getting them to follow your basic house rules. They will have to conform enough so they don't upset your own children. It is to be hoped that in time they will learn to follow the old Roman notion of . . . when with us, do as we do.

When one little girl came to see her remarried father she was told by her stepmother: "You have to go to bed at nine." And she replied: "My mummy lets me go to bed later." What can the new mother do? The weekend mother? This stepmother handled the situation by reaching a compromise. "Now I let her do what she likes—within reason—rather than fighting. There'll be bigger fights later on. I must strengthen myself for that."

Other mothers say:

"I treated his kids like my own. I can't give them one kind of treatment and mine another."

"I act like a mother to his kids when they visit, but sometimes I pull back. I don't want to threaten their relationship with their own mother. I told them that what their mother does doesn't concern me. When they are here they must do what my kids do, or it would not be fair to my children. I can't suspend the rules."

"I feel closest to my own kids but I treat them all fairly. However, they don't come here to be mothered. They come here to see their father for the weekend. I don't try to form an emotional connection. I let them decide how far they want to go."

Each parent has to decide when to insist, when to compromise, and when to give in to children's demands, and whether to make an equal fuss about everything or give in on the less important things. I think, with children, the main point to remember is that when you say something you simply have to stick to it. Children in remarriages will often try to bend you, impress their ways, test you, and one good whack may be worth a thousand words.

Consistency is vital, but it is difficult to sustain when a visiting child goes home and for him things revert to his life-style. One little boy went home after a weekend visit and told his mother that his stepmother had scolded him. The ex-wife called up to complain: "You keep your hands off my child." This boy had apparently begun to lie and to steal from stores, as many disturbed kids will do when they are upset, and the stepmother felt he should be scolded for it. But his real mother refused to believe the story or enforce any punishment. Consistency is necessary, and visiting back and forth between different parents is going to mean that any improvement in behavior will be a long, drawn-out endeavor.

It is particularly rankling when one child is disciplined according to a different set of rules than apply to the other children. A woman explained that her new husband's son was always getting into trouble and doing the wrong thing: "My husband treated him in a way that encouraged him even more. He hardly scolded him at all and actually ended by making excuses for him. But if I commented or offered advice, I was furiously rebuffed. His children were sacred. He felt this way even though he lived with my child, was a complete father to him, and gave him plenty of criticism and punishment when necessary." Lack of discipline or too much permissiveness can wreck the same house as those carloads of toys and candy.

Older children are very aware that, even when they grow to like or love a stepparent, this is not their real parent. And for the stepparent, handing out discipline in a reconstructed family just doesn't come as easily as when the children are there from the beginning. A woman told me that she had to get rid of her stepson's dog because he had bitten a neighbor. The boy was very upset. "He put his fists up against me and threatened to hit me. I was scared. I've always felt the antagonism. It's not personal. It's just that I'm not his mother."

Remarried parents need to agree at the beginning how they will discipline the kids who live with them as well as the kids who don't, and which parent will do it. Both will certainly need a role if it's to be more than a hit-and-miss affair. But if the stepparent is consistently backed up with a firm stamp of approval from the real parent, the children will come to respect both parents and either one will be able to hand out effective chastisement when necessary. Otherwise, retribution will be saved for later on when husband and wife get together, and the disharmony of nightly court appeals and punishments will sour a normally cozy part of the evening.

A New Child

Some remarried people, like many in first marriages, feel that if they have a baby, the child will help cement the bond of marriage. Most people who have new children say that it did help pull everything together for them, though this is certainly a poor reason to have a child when you feel you already have enough. One person told me that sharing the love of a new baby brought her and her new husband and family closer together: "Now all the kids seem closer because, for the first time, they are all related. Since they are all related to the new baby, they are related to each other. No one is left out any more. He's not a threat to anyone because he's a generation lower. There's no rivalry. No secret pinching or punching. They all love him."

"I feel the new baby will tie us all together," a woman remarked. "But I want only one. If we had more children it would make two separate families, while just this one adds something. The new baby can be part of the existing family."

In her study of a hundred families, Dr. Duberman found that in a remarriage where there was a new child, 78 per cent of the families had an excellent relationship; where there was no new child, only 53 per cent had an excellent relationship. It may be true that the baby brought them together or it may simply be that those who are closest decide to have a new baby. Often the decision about a new baby depends on how many children already exist in the remarriage. One couple said they had thought of having a new child, "but we decided four was enough. It was just a romantic notion we had." A woman who felt the same way said that in her second marriage she was more concerned with herself. "I'm selfish about what I'm going to get out of life. We are not going to have more children. Each of us had two and replaced ourselves. I'm physically not capable of going through it again. And four kids to put through college are enough."

The thought of a new baby passes through the minds of most remarried couples. Women who are at all interested in children feel they would like to produce a child with the man they love. A woman told me: "It's crazy, after several years of remarriage I still dream of having a baby. I would like something from the two of us. We talked about it once for two minutes. And that was the end." But having a new child is one of the things that many remarried men and women seem to reject after that initial dream. They usually have enough children, they often don't want a baby in their new lives, and having been through that stage of life, they don't want to return. Besides, remarriage usually brings out the ambitions in middle-class men and women to do something useful, something they really are interested in doing before it's too late. After feeling that life was about over for them, they don't crave more children once they find life giving them one more chance. It is also likely that having had all the children they wanted in the first marriage, and now having had to add to them all the children their new husband or wife wanted in that first marriage (even though those kids may only visit), the collection of children they are responsible for is apt to be twice as many as they had in mind originally. And this is usually enough to dissuade them from creating another person, though the temptation may stay with them for a long time. Good sense prevails over curiosity and desire.

Any Regrets?

Regardless of how much they are adored and enjoyed, the remark I heard most often at the end of every discussion about children was that both parents will be relieved when the kids are grown. They've wanted the experience of children and, for the most part, they have had fun with their kids, but the growing-up period lasts a very long time. People told me, their eyes lighting with anticipation:

"Do I dream? I long for the kids all to be fifty years old."

"I dream of the day my kids are independent. The behavior of my older daughter bugs me."

"When we have fewer kids around it's blissful."

Despite the frequent, complex problems, sometimes the addition of more children in a family can be enriching. Some are pretty well-developed psychologically and they fit in without any tension. But sometimes a stepparent has to work to develop some positive attitudes in the child. Relationships vary along a range from outright hostility to neutral standoffishness, to strong affectionate bonds, and can slide back and forth with the ease of a well-oiled trombone. But no matter whom I spoke to, or what the problems of divorce and remarriage contributed, or how anxious the couple was that the children finally be grown, there were no regrets about the marriage or usually about the children. Some women did say they were sorry they married someone with children, but since those particular men were available only with children, they'd do it again. Another woman admitted: "His kids give us a lot of problems. But I'm not sorry I married him. When you have to solve problems together it brings you closer. We work together to make his little boy happier."

You take on enormous hassles when you remarry someone who has children, but it's hard to regret children whom you know, who exist, who go with the person you want. It might have been easier if the new husband or wife did not have so many dependents, but if there is love in the marriage, the stepparents usually take the kids on as a challenge. They may think of their spouse and feel that by caring for his or her kids, they are doing something helpful for someone they love. And, of course, they may become unusually fond of these stepchildren, sometimes liking them as much as their own kids. A man who had three children in his first marriage, all sons, was absolutely charmed, when he remarried, to add his new wife's two daughters to the household. He liked having young girls around, and although he wasn't attracted to them in a sexual way, he found their physical presence very pleasant. Those who have only girls may enjoy having an extra male around. If the child is anything like the spouse one loves, it is not at all unpleasant to have an extra recipient for the love one feels toward the new spouse. The initial inclination for the woman is to want to love any child of the man she loves. Men may be warier but also feel this way. If there is enough patience and money, and if the children do not come with serious neuroses or learning difficulties, most people accept them with good-natured resignation if not enthusiasm. And eventually life will become simpler for everybody—in any marriage, first, second, or third—when the young ones take off to make their own mistakes, pay for them themselves, and make their own successes.

Even when stepchildren don't fit in as well as they might, most people find forging through the years until they can be alone with each other worth the trouble. The ones who usually find the challenge most difficult are those who never had any children of their own. Yet one childless man I know became an ideal stepfather; he loved to take his stepson skiing, boating, fishing, and he even enjoyed helping him with homework. So much depends on how you feel about children to begin with. But no matter how you feel, the intense devotion generated for a new husband or wife will, in most remarriages, be the deciding factor in whether the whole thing is going to work.

THE
CHILDREN
SPEAK

There have been two common assumptions about the effects of divorce on children. The conventional opinion holds that children forced to witness the breakup of their parents' marriage and the dissolution of family security will be scarred for life by the emotional damage done to them. A more recent assumption is that living in a family constantly torn by strife, argument, and deadly conflict is far worse. In this instance, forced to witness the never-ending pain and cruelty which their parents inflict on each other, being required to exist in a sea of hate and ill-will, children will perceive marriage in a way that will warp their own lives. Not only will they be permanently upset but it will also lessen the possibility that they themselves will ever learn to have a rewarding personal relationship in any marriage they may later enter into.

Many parents who are sensitive to the possibility of harming their kids have clung doggedly to a miserable marriage, devoting their lives to these children, and later they face a wrenching loneliness when the kids grow up and go off to live their own lives. Some people say that since children do not ask to be born, parents (or society) have an obligation to provide them with a happy home, or at least a permanent one, while they are growing up. People also feel that because children are young and innocent, and since they are not responsible for their parents' problems, they should not be forced to suffer because of them. They should be sheltered from any psychological upheaval which will taint them for the rest of their lives. Nevertheless, despite all the concern, ignorance, and controversy about the subject, a million couples divorce a year, most of them with children.

At this difficult emotional time for parents, when accusations fly freely through the air, being accused of destroying the children can be a great burden to carry. It would be useful to know whether the assumptions are valid or not. How seriously and how permanently are children really traumatized? Are the millions of children who are yearly involved in their parents' divorces going to suffer, as a recent editorial in a New York newspaper angrily warned, "emotional and other adverse consequences of wrecked marriages" which will be "even more serious than for the adults involved"?

There can be no doubt that divorce is at first upsetting to children, partly because they do not understand or have not been told the reasons for it. But Dr. Bohannan says that, as far as self-esteem is concerned, he finds no difference in his studies between the children of families that remain together and those in reconstituted families of remarriage. "The kids get to the same place, although by a different road."

Drs. Kenneth L. Wilson, Louis A. Zurcher, and Diana C. McAdams of the Department of Sociology at the University of Texas, and Dr. Russell L. Curtis of the Department of Sociology at the University of Houston, give evidence in a paper* that children survive remarriage better than we think they do. Using data from the 1973 Youth in Transition survey conducted by the Institute for Social Research at the University of Michigan, the Texas researchers tested their own hypothesis that there was no difference between children in stepfather families and those in natural-father families. In this study, over two thousand boys were interviewed in their sophomore year of high school and again three more times during the next five years. The

*Kenneth L. Wilson, Louis A. Zurcher, Diana Claire McAdams, and Russell L. Curtis, "Stepfathers and Stepchildren: An Exploratory Analysis from Two National Surveys," *Journal of Marriage and the Family,* August 1975.

results indicated that one group did not differ from the other in their parental relationships—in terms of discussions about the future, about the possibility of bad grades, or about dropping out of high school. Furthermore, both groups were similar in displaying such characteristics as aggression and delinquent behavior, in expressing a need for self-development, and in feeling a sense of self-esteem and independence. The popular notions that broken families lead to crime and loss of ego were obviously not supported. There are positive and negative factors in both natural and stepparent families, but it would appear that bad behavior cannot be accounted for by divorce and remarriage.

There are certain to be exceptions to the conclusions of any study, and it is probably impossible in a large-scale study to determine exactly how certain problems come into existence, when they do show up, and why they occur. Nevertheless, the surveys are impressive and one is very apt to come away from reading them with the feeling that it is usually better for kids to be with two happy adults than with two adults who spend their hours fighting. The more affection the kids see around them, and receive themselves, the better.

We have already seen examples of the way in which parents react to their own children and to their stepchildren, how they deal with them, and how children change their lives. But there are always at least two sides to any situation involving groups of people, and one should hear them both. Having more insight into how children think should help parents evaluate whether they are doing the right thing with them or making one blunder after another. It's often hard to know just what kids think, even if you confront them in your own family group. They don't always want to display their feelings, and adolescent children are anything but loquacious; they prefer to talk to each other rather than to adults. However, in the following eleven interviews, some written, most oral, the children—some now grown up, some married—seemed eager to say what they truly thought and felt. They knew that no one else would ever know who said what, and they volunteered willingly. Several children declined to be interviewed because they felt the experience of separation from their real parent was still too recent and painful for them, and they had not had enough time to understand what was going on and how they felt about it. These conversations, selected from those I had with children, are in no way meant to be exhaustive. They are relaxed chats, not psychological probings. Some are briefer than others. I let the child determine when he or she had said all he cared to say at the time. I merely hoped to pick up a few helpful clues to the riddle of how divorce and remarriage really affects their lives.

I was curious to know how children felt about several things. One was whether they wished their parents had not divorced, whether, in fact, they thought that parents had the obligation of staying together for the sake of the children, regardless of their own relationship. I also wanted to know how they felt toward a new parent and whether they could ever accept the new marriage.

All the kids I talked to said they thought their parents should have divorced if the marriage was no longer any good. However, they all felt a certain sadness that divorce was necessary. A teen-ager told me: "Intellectually I understand. But down here in my stomach I don't. How can my parents live together so long, love each other and us, and then break up this way?" Since kids often feel that they have caused the divorce in some way, they subconsciously believe they can put it back together again. Consciously, they wish their parents could once again be together, and that the family could be the intimate unit in which they remember growing up. But they know they are probably only imagining how really good things were, and they know the marriage can't be put back together. In spite of all the daydreams and regrets that things didn't stay in one piece, they strongly believe that their parents' decision to divorce was the only possible solution.

Since many parents in the past chose to stay together for the sake of their children, I thought it extremely revealing that, as far as kids are concerned today, these millions of unhappy people may have made the wrong choice. Young children don't yet know much about how human relationships deteriorate, nor are they aware of the intimate details of their parents' difficulties. In fact, parents are sometimes not quite real people to children: they are producers of good meals when one is hungry, of money and authority when one needs them, and, until divorce, parents are thought of as permanent fixtures. Like the Rock of Gibraltar, a parent is always there. I think that, if parents were to convey their thoughts and feelings more frequently to their children, the reasons for divorce—or whatever else it is that parents choose—would make more sense.

One man I knew did stay with his wife for twenty-seven years. He was fairly religious and a family man, and he thought he was doing the right thing. After all those years of sticking out a bad family situation, in which he had sacrificed his chances for a better life and happiness with someone else, he finally asked his grown son whether staying with his mother (whom he had at last divorced) had been the best thing for all of them, even though the atmosphere in the house was not always the most cheerful. The boy replied: "Dad, you didn't do us any favors."

In talking to the many children I met I tried to set forth a few basic questions and keep the discussion short. These are some of the questions I asked:

—How do you feel about your parent's remarriage?

—What don't you like about your new father or mother?

—What do you miss about the way it used to be?

—Is the new family better or worse than your original family?

—Are you envious of kids whose parents are still together?

—Should parents stay together for the sake of the kids?

—How do you feel about your stepbrothers and stepsisters?

—Are you jealous of the time your parent spends with the new mother or father?

—Do you think your mother or father is happier now?

Some children had nothing to say on certain subjects and seemed to want to talk about other things which they did have opinions about. I let the interviews flow where they would.

Case One

S., who is now married, in her thirties, with two children, has gone back to school and is getting a graduate degree. Her husband works for the State Department. She was a senior in college when her parents were divorced, and her sister was eleven years old.

"I knew things had been strained for at least three or four years before the divorce. My mother had been unhappy and drank too much. My father moved to an upstairs apartment in the house. But my younger sister didn't realize anything was wrong. She was surprised when Dad moved out but just thought her family was a bit peculiar, maybe a bit unhappy, and she accepted what they did. Kids always go along with the way parents operate. But I was very aware of their unhappiness. I think sex might have had something to do with it, but as a child you never know that. Their fights were behind closed doors. They were cold, lacked affection. But I didn't mind at the time. I didn't have enough experience with other families to appreciate the difference. I just accepted the way it was. The thing I worried about was what would happen to me if they split. I didn't worry about them. I had my own anxieties and feelings. They finally were divorced.

"I was over twenty-one when my mother remarried. All of us were there. Her daughters and a granddaughter were at the wedding. Mother married a nice, quiet man who doesn't bother her. I like him. Mother hadn't really wanted the divorce. It was a big blow to her. She felt she had been discarded. She would rather my father had stayed and they had stayed miserable. As for me, I think it was better that they split. But they should have done it sooner so that I would not have had to grow up in an atmosphere where there was no love. I don't think parents should stay together for the sake of their kids. What kind of people will children become if life is arranged so perfectly for them? Why sacrifice for the kids? I know my father is happier now. Mother certainly is. Why did they wait?"

Case Two

C. is now in her twenties and is unmarried but living with a man. She is a public-relations agent for a theater. One of three children, she was thirteen when her parents divorced and fourteen when her father remarried. Her mother remarried six years later.

"Their divorce was unexpected. There were no warning signs, no yelling and screaming. It was all undercover until one day Dad just came to me and said, 'Your mother has asked me to leave the house.' We all jumped on Mother and said, 'We hate you.' The divorce took place. And we saw Dad every Sunday—which was easy because we lived only three blocks from each other. They never explained why they were divorced. We haven't been told to this day why. I instantly liked my stepmother. But when my mother remarried I was shocked. After the divorce I had been taking care of my mother and continued for six years. She was my best friend. She always came to me and told me things. When she remarried, it wasn't children's hour any more when she came home from work. It was adults' hour.

"I didn't like the idea also because it meant leaving where we lived.

But I knew she wanted to be with someone. We were getting older. So I accepted it. I like my stepfather, but he is different from my father. I do sometimes wish my parents were together again. It goes through my head. All kids who have divorced parents think of it at one time or another. They wish their parents could be married again. But they shouldn't stay together for the sake of the kids. If they do, you can get to hate a parent. I have friends whose parents stayed and it's wicked on them. It's never healthy for the kids. You are always aware of an undercurrent floating around the house, so you don't want to go home. Parents are human beings and need to have good lives too.

"My stepmother has two kids of her own. She is sort of weak physically, and when we visit and things have to be done, she asks us to do it rather than her own kids. If there is dog-do on the rug we have to clean it. But we are all close and good friends and keep in touch. There is a lot of love there. My stepmother became a good friend and never tried to mother me.

"In a way I'm glad my parents didn't tell me everything. If I'd known each one's story I might find different interpretations of each of their actions. I might find out things I'd rather not know.

"Our family was raised on love. We always kissed and showed affection. My stepfather was just not part of that kind of family. He was not used to outwardly showing love. I wasn't willing to accept the marriage right away. Now I love and respect him. I realize not everyone is the same.

"I do miss the close relationship I had with my mother, and I really appreciate it when I am all alone with her. But in the house, my stepparent isn't an outsider. I think the younger the kid, the easier it is to accept remarriage. The longer you live with a parent, the more he becomes a part of your life. If you are much older, you might be going off to college and never even get to know your stepparent.

"One of the things I miss most is my parents' cocktail hour. They'd come home from work and have a drink and we'd always talk and the stereo was on and they'd always be dancing.

"Mom is happier now than between marriages. But that period made her more independent and stronger. I sometimes fantasize that my parents might get married again. But knowing them now I don't think it would work in a million years.

"When I go home with friends and their parents are still married

I think it's kind of nice. Friends say, 'Oh you poor thing, you must have had such a rough life.' But it's a fact of life. I don't worry about it.

"I don't like to use the name 'step' mother or father. In introductions I don't like to say this is my mother and this is my stepfather. It sort of puts him down.

"I like my stepfather's three daughters. But with the one who is my age, we are a threat to each other and we always competed. At the beginning of their marriage, I was jealous of the time my new father spent with my mother. I do feel a sort of favoritism. My stepfather is exuberant when his kids come home. And my mother and stepmother are more concerned with taking care of the house and more willing to let their own kids have guests over rather than their stepkids. But I think we work things out well. I just don't let the occasional thoughtlessness bother me."

Case Three

G. is a sophomore in high school and suddenly getting good grades after a poor beginning. He was six years old when his parents were divorced and is an only child.

"I was so young when my parents were divorced, I don't remember much about my father. And I never got to know him because he just disappeared from our lives. He is married and living in another state and never visits. I don't feel envious of kids whose parents are not divorced because divorce didn't hurt me. My mother remarried a year after the divorce and I have a new father whom I think of as my father. I use his last name, though of course it isn't legal.

"I don't think parents should stick together because of the child. It seems to me that parents don't normally do something because the child is there. It's up to the parents to do what they want to do. If I were a parent I would. Kids are more independent now anyway and can manage if their parents break up. I think if my parents divorced now, when I am fifteen, I might hate it. But they still should be able to do what they want. I don't miss my first father at all. I like my stepbrother and stepsister. They are older and have never lived with us. My mother is happier. I know because she told me. I like where we live better. I'm happier."

Case Four

C. is fourteen and plans to be a teacher or psychologist someday. She has a sister who is eleven and crazy about horses. Her parents separated two years ago and are now divorced.

"It didn't upset me a whole lot. They never had the same viewpoint on anything. If one of them wanted to go somewhere early, the other one would want to arrive late. After they separated I realized even more how much of this I'd been seeing.

"I've always felt closer to my mother—I guess because my father is around less often. My father is now living with Missy and I don't know whether they will get married. I just call her by her first name. She fit perfectly into my life. It's hard to explain. I really like her. She's not like my mother at all. She seems to be full of life and knows so much about so many things. Sometimes it's hard to imagine that Dad loves another woman, but it doesn't bother me. I like Missy so much, it would seem a pity if she'd never come into my life.

"I see Dad every weekend. They live in the same town. We sometimes spend the night there when Mom goes away for the weekend. I get along better with Missy than with my father. He's too critical. He's a bit different than before. He's more anxious to do things when we see him. He's too worried about what we're thinking of him. He should relax. He tries too hard sometimes.

"At first, when they separated, I didn't take sides. Then for a short time I thought, He's leaving Mummy. Then I realized she was leaving him, too. No, I don't wish they could be married again. They're happier divorced. It doesn't bother me particularly. I'm concerned with my own life. I see my father enough. If they're happier this way it's fine. Sometimes I miss not being a whole family. I miss the big parties we'd have when we'd sit around and grab the dips and talk to people. Mother's parties aren't as big now.

"Parents should not stay together for the sake of the kids. They have to live their own lives, too. They have just as much responsibility to themselves as they do to their kids. But if they are getting divorced, they have to try to make it as fair and unhard on the kids as possible by discussing it with their kids. And they should not do anything silly, like having jealous tantrums or refusing to talk to each other.

"I'm never jealous of Missy. But once in a while little things bother me a bit. When we're visiting, Dad will say, 'Oh, don't eat all that. Leave some for Missy.' It doesn't make me jealous, it just makes me annoyed at my father. It's not often. Just little things sometimes. I know he loves us as much as he ever did.

"I'll probably get married someday, but I'm not sure. I mean I don't think it's necessary to be actually married. Maybe I'll just live with someone. Even if I marry I'll certainly live with someone first, long enough to know his little habits that could drive you up the wall. You have to know if you could function day-to-day.

"I'd like to have two children, not more. The population can't take it. Just enough to replace ourselves. And I'll always work. Both of us will."

Case Five

R. was eleven years old when his mother remarried. He is now nineteen and in college.

"I had mixed feelings about my mother's remarrying. I liked my stepfather. But we were moving and I was sad to leave my real father. I never realistically wish my parents were together again—but once in a while . . . It was a bad scene before. My father had remarried, too. I didn't like his new wife. She was materialistic. I'm different. But now we get along. I do think parents should get a divorce when they are not getting along. Staying together for the sake of the children is not for the sake of the children at all. Parents sometimes have a closer relationship with a kid after a divorce. My father made time to see me. My new father is different than my real dad. He doesn't say what he feels all the time. He keeps things inside. I never know quite how he feels. In restaurants he jokes loudly and does what my real father wouldn't approve of. He sometimes makes me feel uncomfortable. My real father and new father are so opposite. One is proper and the other is casual. It doesn't confuse me too much. I learned to act the way they want me to. I adapt to each of them.

"At first I was excited about having a new brother, but all of a sudden I had to share my room. We are different. We fought all the time. I was stubborn and got what I wanted. He kept things inside and didn't talk. My real brother, who was thirteen then, and my stepbrother used to fight all the time. I also didn't like having to share my mother. Sometimes I still wish it were just the three of us. My mother, my real brother and me. There were days when my mother would go off with just one of us and do what that child wanted to do. We finally decided to have family meetings to sort out the problems between all the kids. It helped. As the months went on, there was less and less to talk about. I am closest to my real brother. I can't be with my stepbrother too long. But I do think we have succeeded in forming one family. Our new family is better, I have to admit. Everyone is happier. My brother and I used to be aware of my parents fighting every night. Everything has turned out okay in the end. In fact, sometimes I feel lucky to have more than two parents. The majority of my friends' parents have been divorced.

"As for playing favorites, every once in a while I feel my stepfather treats his own kids better. He's defensive about them. Perhaps he isn't really treating them better. But I just feel he is.

"I imagine that I will get married someday. I'd probably like to live with the woman first. When you're dating it's not like being married. When you live together you find out if there are things that might drive you crazy. But the thought of living with only one person all my life turns my stomach. I guess I believe in marriage because of the security it offers. You can't just marry a person you love. You have to be able to get along with her. There must be compatibility. There's got to be lots of compromising. Not yourself. But your ideas. You have to be able to each express yourself and do what the other one wants to do.

"My parents got married when they were eighteen and twenty-one. And they grew in different directions. They didn't have enough in common. There is nothing wrong with not marrying and just living together, but if there are kids, getting married avoids a lot of hassles. I'd want a ceremony. I'm a romanticist. Maybe it's the symbolism. A friend of mine lived with a fellow for two years and then got married. She now regrets it. All of a sudden she felt she was a wife. It changed how they felt toward each other.

"Another friend I have got married at eighteen. I thought he was too young. But I couldn't begin to tell him why, to tell him all the things I knew, and he wouldn't have understood anyway. I think most children of divorce can learn from their parents' experience. Some will repeat their parents' mistakes."

Case Six

D. was eight when her parents separated. She is now sixteen and is about to enter college with top grades. She lives with her father and stepmother.

"I think marriage is a fraud. It's not what it's made out to be. As I see it now, when I look around at the people who are married, it's an unequal relationship. The man is still in control. I can't see, if I were married, having to worry about both my job and the grocery list. My other objection to marriage is the state of mind of faithfulness. I don't like having to be faithful to one other person. Physically and mentally, there is just one life to live. I want to experience as much as I can. I don't think people should feel guilty if they are unfaithful sexually.

"When my parents were divorced, I felt hurt. I felt my father was leaving me, too, not just my mother. I saw him four times a month, every Tuesday. Now I'd regret it if my father and mother got together again. They're happy without each other. My mother developed so much as a person when she was divorced. She just blended into the decor before. Now I see each of my parents as so much more of an individual. My mother has become my best friend. Kids whose parents stay together don't see their mother and father as individuals.

"I was very deeply hurt by my father's remarriage and by my mother's living with a fellow for the last seven years. I felt jealous. I had to compete for both my father's and my mother's affections. I still am jealous. Mother doesn't marry because she doesn't want to be tied down. My stepmother has become a great friend and I love her very much. My mother thinks my stepmother is neurotic and she didn't want me to live with them because they have emotional problems. I wanted to live with my father and came here anyway. But my mother wouldn't give up the support checks. My stepmother told her to either give up the checks or I couldn't stay with them. My mother refused to give up the money. I was having a family romance with my father and hated my mother for saying no. So my stepmother kicked me out and she has felt guilty about it ever since. It took about six years for everyone to straighten out. And now I'm back with my father.

"I'd get married someday if we each could do our own thing. We each have every right to do what we want whether married or not. I suppose my parents' experience has affected me. I can see it, especially now with my father and stepmother. When they are together they are faithful. Okay. But when they are separated they both fool around. It works. I've got to draw my own conclusions. My mother always told me I'm a free individual.

"I'm a bit cynical about my father's second marriage. I don't think he knows what marriage is. That's the whole problem. You go into it with expectations. I think he could get married ten times and he'd never know. Everyone has some unreal expectations. But I think I'll be able to cope and adjust because of my experience."

Case Seven

M. is seventeen and ready to go off to college next year. Her parents have been divorced for about four years. She and a younger brother stayed with her mother. An older brother and sister went to live with her father. Later, she too moved in with her father.

"I was thirteen when my parents were divorced, and I was not aware they had had any conflict. At the time I thought it wouldn't bother me. But I realize now it upset me a lot. I like the people each one of them has married. If they'll accept me as a friend, and not try to be my mother or father, I will like my stepparents.

"Sometimes I wish my parents could be married to each other again. I know it's totally impractical, but when I see them together, it flashes through my mind. I've had to adapt to my stepparents. They're different. My stepfather is sterner and quiet. My stepmother is emotional, while my real mother is more self-contained. My stepmother uses frozen foods and doesn't buy expensive cereals I like. My real mother is a gourmet cook. There's more discipline at my stepmother's. I like the discipline but there are problems. For example, my stepmother wouldn't let me wash my clothes unless I filled the washer. But at my mother's I find them too family-oriented. We all had to eat together. I am not interested in family to that extent. In that sense I feel freer at my stepmother's. She accepts me as an adult.

"I had been thinking of leaving my mother and moving to my father's for several years and it finally happened. I was baking a cake for a friend and my mother insisted it had to be for the family, even though I'd bought all the materials with my own money. So I left home.

"I really can accept the remarriage. As I grew up I began to see the differences between my parents. They are exactly opposite to each other. The thing I miss most is not being able to live with all my brothers and my sister. I think once in a while it would be great if my parents were still together, but I realize most of my friends' parents are not doing so well. I don't think parents should stay together for the sake of the kids. No, that's worse. That's how you screw up kids. It's just sad that they didn't catch it before they had children. It's worse to let it go.

"I love my stepbrothers. But my little brother is jealous of them. I felt a bit strange about my mother having sex with a man who is not my father, but they were careful. I think my parents are happier now, and any problems they have are not because of whom they married but are things they have to work out in their own heads.

"When they were divorced, each parent told me the mean things the other had done. I was in the middle. There should be a place kids can go during divorce. Parents are each trying to get support from the child. I didn't want contact with either of them. They were each trying to tell me things. I told them I didn't want to hear. I said it often enough so they got the idea.

"I have a strong sense of who my mother and father are. I'd resent anyone else taking over their roles. If my stepmother did, I'd be nasty or I'd withdraw and be cold. I want her just to be a friend."

Case Eight

R. is now in his thirties, is an editor, and is married with two children. His parents divorced when he was only two years old and his mother never remarried.

"My father remarried and they had twin daughters; he moved away and I never saw him. But I never gave it any thought. I eventually went to boarding school, and when you meet with your peers in that situation, parents are not important. I couldn't tell you whether many of my friends had sisters or brothers or mothers and fathers. My mother never spoke about my father and I didn't think about him. I was so young when he left, I don't remember him. It would be worse to have had a perfect relationship with him and then lose it. The fact that you don't have this relationship and others do doesn't bother you. You don't envy them. After all, others have Rolls-Royces and you don't.

"Actually not having a father affected me more practically than emotionally. It was inconvenient not to have him there to hit a ball with me or teach me things like carpentry. Growing up in a female environment spoiled me.

"When I was between thirteen and eighteen I was very influenced by a male teacher. I even chose history as my major because I was interested in him. He was sparkling, fascinating. I think anything I have I got from him. When we were free in the afternoon after classes, we went to his house. And he exposed us to ideas. My mother was not like that. She was very practical.

"My father never saw me. Perhaps it was laziness or because he thought it was the best thing to do; he never contacted me. Maybe he thought it was best to leave things as they were. He is not outgoing. But I never felt deprived.

"I was twenty-six and about to be married when I went to see him. I liked his wife. She was very pleasant. The thing that struck me was that if I saw him in the street there was nothing to tell me he was my father. We don't look alike. If not for the facts, I never would have known him. I said to myself, 'This is my father,' but I didn't get any kick out of it. We spent half a day together and he talked mainly about boats, which are his hobby.

"I don't feel that the situation of my parents has had a negative effect on me. So if my marriage was not going well, I'd get a divorce if I had to. If people are thinking of separating but can't make up their minds, and if there are children, then I think the children should influence you. But I don't think people should stay married if they don't want to. I think children are usually influenced by their parents' problems and their parents' hysteria, and not directly affected by things themselves. They react to the way their parents react. They can take whatever happens.

"I believe in marriage. I think it's rough for one parent to bring up a child alone. It's just easier with two. There are so many things you can trade off."

Case Nine

N. is now in her twenties, a graduate of an art school, and a busy painter. She was fifteen when her mother died. Her father, who has two other daughters, was married six months later to a woman who also has children.

"I felt a great loss when my mother died. I resented my father's new wife and I was very critical of my father and jealous of her. Of course now I'm glad he married. I want him to be happy. At the time I was thinking of my own needs. I was used to certain standards. My stepmother did things differently, and I resented the changes. Rationally I could deal with it, but emotionally I couldn't. I had to get used to her personality. She was more open and affectionate than my mother. My mother was more austere. They had different ways of expressing themselves.

"All the kids got along well. My stepmother had two daughters in high school. Her kids at least had their father somewhere, so for them there was no sense of loss. But we had lost our mother and it was harder to relate to a new parent. I interpreted everything as being against me. And seeing him with another woman was difficult. If my father's marriage had broken up or I had seen it decline, I would have realized they weren't compatible. But it didn't. They were in love. When there were problems, her kids could go back to their father, but I had nowhere else to go—they had an alternative; I had no other parent to turn to. They could and did manipulate their parents to get what they wanted. I couldn't.

"It was sad for me to see the house redecorated. It was sad to see things go. Also, Father picked up certain affectations from his new wife and it bothered me to see him changing. They talked baby talk. He began it. It aggravated me. When I was irritated, everything mattered. For example, my stepmother worked. On the way home she would pick up a bag of frozen chopped onions. I saw this as symbolic of her lack of caring. My mother would never have done this. My mother would have minced fresh onions. If I ever became mad, I'd think of the onions. I argued, I fought, I yelled at them both. I was just full of my own sorrow. Now, five years later, I can understand and love them both."

Case Ten

C. is now in her twenties, married to a graduate student, and works in a museum. She was a student in high school when her parents divorced. Her mother did not remarry, but her father married a woman with a young son. C. asked me if she could write down her thoughts, which follow:

"I have always thought of divorce as a positive, viable action. Even when it occurred in my family, I believed that divorce (and perhaps eventual remarriage) could be a constructive attempt to resolve an incompatible relationship. Two adults have every right (particularly if the children involved are full-grown, which I think makes the decision easier) to think of their own happiness first. Too often parents, mothers especially, sacrifice their individuality and devote every energy and attention to the children's needs. People and needs change over the years and marriage is too often entered into without sufficient foresight.

"Remarriage introduces complications. The new family requires patience and effort to make it work. It is a challenge. The stepmother is confronted with the onerous burden of making peace with her husband's children. She must establish her identity and, should she be so ambitious, establish a rapport with the children. This process involves an attempt to understand the background of the child and become familiar with former, childhood relationships between children and parents. It is an enormous undertaking. One can never reconstruct the past (unless you are a trained psychologist). All the influences and circumstances are never recovered. The pieces rarely fit. The result is too often a distorted, inaccurate portrayal of the nuclear family. Based upon her eventually understanding the children's make-up, needs, and sensitivities, the stepmother might then try to find a niche in that picture for herself. This is the ideal stepmother—someone thoughtful and interested enough to actively attempt to seek and establish acceptance in a 'foreign' environment. It's an enormous task that I hope never to confront—what an impossible, frustrating job!

"Then, of course, the children must figure out how to regard and accept the stepmother. (I hate that word stepmother.) Should she be a friend, a second mother, both, something else? With lots of luck and hard work the aims and beliefs of the stepmother and children will mesh into a successful, enjoyable relationship!

"Once upon a time . . . The summer of 1968 I was a counselor at camp, and recall having eight campers in my cabin, and six of these girls came from 'broken' homes. This was quite disturbing to me, particularly because the kids were literally deposited at camp for the summer, against their own will. Anyway, when I returned home that August, I remember remarking to Mom and Dad about this phenomenon. How ironic indeed when later that year I was told of my own parents' decision to divorce. I must admit I was surprised, shocked. I don't recall ever questioning their right to do so or thinking of it in terms of myself and their responsibility to me. But the event, separation and divorce, was unexpected to me. (Perhaps this indicates the lack of communication in our household.)

"I think that during my high school years and before, I was quite a conscientious and relatively mature individual. I enjoyed responsibility and was fairly broadminded, considering my limited experiences. However, when I was informed of the divorce and expected to function as a sort of 'go-between,' the strain mounted. It was tough to digest the opinions, feelings of each parent, to evaluate and comprehend objectively the crisis that these two adults were experiencing. It was hard to air my emotions or hear other people's viewpoints which might have served to reduce the divorce to realistic, manageable proportions. I adjusted, though. Senior year was a busy, demanding time. I would be leaving home the next year anyway, so it didn't critically affect me. I was happy to learn that Dad was remarried. He was so miserable living in that dreary house alone after the separation. I don't think he could ever make it as a bachelor.

"My reactions to my stepmother? I was duly impressed with her cosmopolitan credentials. She appeared to me first (and now) as an attractive, intelligent, aggressive career woman, the likes of which I'd never met before. My reaction to her was cautious. She was confident and came on strong. I didn't quite know how to relate to a 'stepmother.' But more than that, I sincerely believe that my response was not a conscious reaction to her as stepmother, but to her as an unusual personality. I tend to assess people in terms of myself. This is a natural self-comparison to formulate a perspective. But it was at first a little difficult to identify with her, since we are not much alike. Perhaps another factor enters into play here. I met her at a turning point in my life. As a college student, I had reached a critical period when I was expected to make decisions regarding my own future, plan for a career. Not knowing what I wanted to do and being noncommittal, I was a bit defensive and feeling guilty about my ambivalence. Her accomplishment in the professional realm reinforced my own insecurities. I felt somewhat threatened.

"I remember our chats and our decision to be friends; this was to be the basis of our new relationship. Great! A second mother would never do—one mother is plenty! This would also complement the new relationship that I was developing with Dad.

"I think the only difficulty arises when she becomes bogged down in my problems. If Dad is troubled about something, she becomes understandably and unfortunately involved. He invites her opinion, an alternative viewpoint, but she cannot remain objective. It's impossible. It would be better, in my opinion, if she didn't try to advise me, unless I solicited her help. I suppose we all reach a point in our lives when we no longer want to be treated as children. It's bad enough to receive criticism from a parent, who will always be a parent and consider it his right and duty to dole out advice. Everyone needs advice, like it or not. But not from anyone else.

"There is one other issue which I think Dad already understands. I don't play favorites with parents. I love Dad and Mom for their very different and wonderful qualities and quirks. Dad now has a new life that is fulfilling and happy. My mother lives alone, doesn't travel or have pressing social commitments. For these reasons and the fact that she is my mother and daughters are naturally closer to their mothers, I stay with Mom when I drift through town. It's more convenient. Dad sympathizes with this, even though I don't see him as much."

Case Eleven

J. is fifteen now and goes to a prep school in the town where he lives, but he was only a little boy when his father died and his mother remarried. It has taken him eight years to readjust. This is how he set it down on paper for me:

"When I was seven years old my father died. This is the reason for the shock and the trauma that erased seven years of my life. Things could have cleared up a lot quicker if my mother had not decided to marry again. But she did remarry, and I had a new father.

"Perhaps the mistake I made when I first lived with my stepfather was trying to accept him and believe that he was my new father. From the start I worked the image of my stepfather into something which he could not be. When he failed to meet my expectations, I immediately took it out on him and everyone surrounding me. This was the beginning of a conflict which would last for many years. I built a wall between me, my family and friends. I could not accept my stepfather for what he really was, just a person who was married to my mother. The emotional effects on me were devastating. I no longer cared about anyone or anything. I turned inward, trying to escape the world as it really was. Conflicts with my stepfather occurred frequently. I am not saying that he was the only one to blame for them; however, I didn't give my stepfather even half a chance. This combination of emotional events, plus the fact that I was physically weak, made me a stifled person. In school I was extremely intelligent and liked by all the teachers; but my work habits became lazy and I just didn't care. I needed a change, and I needed it quickly.

"At the time I lived in Long Island. I had lived in the same town since I was three. This atmosphere had accompanied me through all my emotional traumas. Perhaps the change I needed was a move to a different place. At the time I could not see this, and I hated my stepfather even more when he announced that we were moving. I was scared, shy, outraged, and confused when we moved. Life seemed even more looming and depressing. As I look back now, I can see that this move was the best medicine that I could have possibly had. Now I was in a new town, a new life-style. Would things change? At first it was frightening. I wondered how I would make new friends. I didn't think that people would accept me. For the first year, things didn't change much. My stepfather still aggravated me, and my schoolwork was still falling far behind my potential. This time, however, I was not a defeatist. I didn't draw back into my own little secluded world which I had created for my emergencies. Something made me want to try; I don't know whether it was the new atmosphere, or whether I was beginning to realize things as they truly were. In any case, life began to improve.

Case Eleven   *117*

"The events which happened in the next two years bring me up to the present. In those two years I have accomplished much. For the first time I realized that my stepfather was never trying to act as my father. My relations with him have improved greatly and are still improving. On the other side, my schoolwork has jumped from average grades to the honor roll; and, most important, I have friends who truly care about me as I also care about them. In this period of two years from age thirteen to fifteen my life entirely changed. As I have mentioned, it improved mentally, socially, and much to my delight, physically. A big jump from the person I was.

"In retrospect, I ask myself 'Why? How did I improve?' I suppose that I am a very lucky person. If I had remained on Long Island, none of the opportunities that I have taken would have been opened to me. I can truthfully say that it was by no outside help that my condition improved. Everything I have today is because I wanted it to be. However, I must also recognize my mother as a great promoter of ideals. Without her, a lot of things would not have happened.

"Finally, I can look at all aspects of my past life from an objective point of view. My old life is dead, even though some vestiges still remain. These vestiges are various feelings which I still hold. I will always wonder what it would have been like if my father had lived. I still feel cheated in losing him. However, what has happened has happened. The many years of emotional strife have turned into endless years of mental insight. The experience has enriched me and turned me into the person I am today. My only great mistake was to take my stepfather and expect him to pick up where my father left off. Deep inside, I knew that this was, and always will be, impossible."

These few case histories offer some insight into some of the things which children worry over when their parents change the context in which they have lived. It's a completely new world after divorce, and children's responses have to change to keep pace with it. Their thoughts on what it does to them are self-explanatory. But several points appear more than once.

Most kids whose parents divorced were shocked by the event. They may have been suspicious that all was not right, they may have gotten used to the fights, but no one warned them that a breakup was being contemplated until it had been decided. From what they say, children need to know more about what's going on in their homes between their parents. Divorce would be much less of a shock and easier to swallow if parents explained in the early stages that they are having problems and may not be able to go on living together.

Children also seem to approve of divorce as early as necessary. They don't like living in a tension-filled atmosphere, and adjustment seems to be easier when they don't remember much because the breakup came when they were young.

Although all the children I spoke to had daydreams of seeing their original parents back together again, none of them realistically wanted it or thought it could work. They understand divorce and the need for it far more acutely than their parents gave them credit for. If parents simply told kids the straightforward facts without blame or embellishment, kids could absorb the truth far more easily than the embroidered version of half-truth and coverup that they get. A few more factual man-to-man chats and a little less protection from reality, and kids would be able to handle what their parents come up with and not suffer quite as much.

Children sense favorites in blended families, and parents should make an effort to treat all the kids living with them in the same way, though at times it is difficult or even inappropriate. At least they should be spoken to in the same tone of voice, receive the same punishment, the same kind of gifts, and the same privileges from both parents.

The passage of time—both for the kids whose parents divorce and for those whose one parent dies—is essential. This is something they just have to live through, and those who mentioned the length of time it took them indicated that it was at least five years. It may take this long and even longer for their emotions to comprehend what their intellect understood immediately.

While in all probability most kids make some sort of successful adjustment to the new situation, there are children who never will. It is very likely that these children had psychological insecurities or other problems before the divorce and remarriage took place and they simply refuse to accept reality. They become rebellious, unsympathetic, and they stay that way, never fully accepting the new marriage. The number of children in this category is probably quite small; yet the problems exist and can cause sadness in a family. But it should be remembered that—even in a natural family—some children grow into extremely independent adults and don't see their parents very often. However, the child who passes judgment on a parent and stepparent, and tries to penalize those who decide to live differently than he would have them live, is making mistakes which hurt the new couple.

Remarriage after a divorce may be easier for some kids to accept than a remarriage after the death of a parent. Much depends on how the parent who leaves the household in divorce behaves.

And, finally, it is heartening and rather important to note that children don't have the innocence their parents had at the same age. Each generation seems to grow up and be increasingly sophisticated at an earlier age. These kids of divorce and remarriage, and probably all kids of their generation, are not all sure they will marry, do not plan to marry young, and are refreshingly open to new ideas. In talking to them, I found it difficult to imagine them entering into marriage with the same naïve expectations or childlike unworldliness that a lot of their parents did. I don't doubt that the growing numbers of children who do have stepparents, or let's call them belle-parents or beta-parents (the alphas were first), will have learned from their own parents' experience that marriage can be either tragic or beautiful.

THE
REWARDS
OF MARRIAGE

Every time we take action, we make waves. For every action, there are costs and there are benefits. In economics, cost-benefit analyses are constantly being examined to decide whether something is worth doing or not, whether the benefits are worth the costs, the goods worth the bads.

The majority of couples I questioned agreed that remarriage was worth the costs they had to pay. The weight of all the advantages that remarriage brought far exceeded the weight of all the problems, no matter how complex or unexpected. In fact, a number of men and women regretted that they could not have had their second marriage first, and enjoyed it from the beginning. (Whether it could have been the same as a first marriage, however, is doubtful.) They were sorry they had wasted so many years growing up, learning about life and themselves, living through earlier mistakes, now making it impossible for them to have the long, blissful marriage they would like to have with their second partner. They regretted that this second marriage would last only twenty or thirty years instead of forty or fifty.

You See What You Are Getting

One of the important ways a second marriage differs from a first is that the days of being a novice adult, not knowing who one is or where one is going, are largely over. Both partners are more experienced at marriage by now, which means that everything moves more smoothly, more meaningfully. At least one of the two, and possibly both, are launched on a career, so that there is greater economic security. And both bring to the marriage a multitude of refreshingly new habits, interests, talents, and ideas. What each person is getting in the marriage is more easily defined; it can be seen and evaluated. There is less guessing. Each person has formed his habits, his way of life is a familiar routine, his bank account is visible. She has already decided whether she likes children and homemaking or a career. He has already decided whether he is going to be a doctor who works all hours at a hospital or does research from nine to five. And each person has survived and been molded by his past marriage. In each remarriage, knowing what he or she did not want in life has helped to define more clearly what he or she *does* want.

Not only are the career, bank account, style of life, and habits obvious and easy to evaluate but a person's character and personality are fully developed. In the mélange of postcollege job-hunting and parties, it's hard to see through the fun-loving, youthful haze which way one's friends are going to go. With a little time, will they become jolly or nagging, will they pick on small details or wait for the larger things to upset them? Will they be demanding or helpful? Grumpy or even-tempered? Moody or pleasant and understanding? These traits are usually not obvious and need time to unfold themselves in the maturing adult, and only later on will they be fully observable, when people are older and take themselves more seriously. Most people marry for the first time before these vital signs are apparent. The second time, one sees exactly what one is getting: rich, poor, fat, thin, mean, gentle, bald, hairy. A lover of the city or one who dotes on country life. One who prefers to be surrounded by modern furniture or a connoisseur of antiques. One who likes his shirts starched hard or a devotee of soft, wrinkly shirts. One who cooks well or one who simply cooks. One who drinks too much, enough, or not at all or who goes bananas about the correct Bordeaux vineyard and knows the best vintages. A night person, a day person, a sloppy person, a neat person, a sports nut, an opera fan, an outdoor type, an indoor type. Whatever he or she is, you have a better idea of what you're getting (and what you're giving) the second time around. It is easier to choose someone who is more like you, and with whom you are more likely to enjoy life.

Is Remarriage Happier?

The happiness described by the men and women I spoke to was an awesome and impressive outpouring, especially considering the fact that I chose my remarried sample quite randomly. I did not look for *happily* remarried people, just for *remarried* people. Thus their unanimous gladness and satisfaction with life came as a surprise. I would have thought that in a randomly chosen sample there would have been some who regretted what they did, some who were on the verge of failure, some who buckled under all the pressures of remarriage and were about to give up. It wasn't so. There were problems, but there was an invisible wall of happiness that seemed to separate these people from a lot of other married people. One might expect them to say their second marriages were happier because they were comparing their newfound happiness with a marital fiasco. But even on further probing, when I asked them to remember the early days of their first marriages, even though it was hard to remember clearly what one felt like some years ago, their unwavering and unanimous impression was that the second marriage had it all over the first one in terms of pure, deep happiness. It is true that one's first love (not always the person they married) and one's first sex experience (again, not always the person they married) are both unforgettable, but the excitement of the first marriage, the feeling of being in love—if they had it the first time —did not last very long and more often they quickly became disillusioned. They said they had never found the lasting, profound, committed happiness they wanted until their second try. Those I talked to had been married varying lengths of time, but most had been married long enough the second time for cracks in the shining surface to begin to show. It seemed to prove that although things might end by dissolving someday, for a variety of reasons, these people had found a serious and long-lasting relationship that they were enjoying and getting a lot out of. This, they said, was more than they ever had in their first marriages. At times their assurances of good fortune were positively effusive.

One woman bubbled: "Complicated? Yes. But happiness! I never in my youngest, most romantic days dreamed of anything like this. We are unbelievably close."

"My second marriage is happier," another woman assured me. "The first time I never thought about it. It just happened. I got married, had two kids, here I am. Now what. Trapped. This time I'm ecstatic."

A young woman confided: "I've never been so happy. We both feel we are enormously lucky. We often wonder if there are others in the world as happy. He feels every single need I have. I don't think this would have been possible when I was young. At twenty-three I didn't know what it was like to be married. The first time, marriage is like buying a pig in a poke. You can't possibly know what marriage means."

In effect, this woman was saying that the kind of happiness she wanted and needed to have with a man was something that would have been impossible to choose, recognize, or create when she was younger. Of course, whether this intense happiness that people feel is simply due to the maturity of being older, or the experiences they've had, is an open question. It is impossible to say whether it comes from what they learned when they had their fingers (or hearts) burned or whether it comes with age and its mellowing influence, making people more tolerant and philosophical. Or, for that matter, whether they could find what they wanted because the social climate has changed. Women said they are happier now, especially because they are taken more seriously.

"My second marriage is infinitely happier than my first. There is an acceptance of me as a person, the way I am. My first husband wanted to change me."

"I feel that I can be myself. In my first marriage I used to feel I was walking on eggshells. Now if I crack a few shells it doesn't matter. I am more alive in my second marriage. In my first, I felt a woman had to assume a definite role. I was supposed to defer to my husband. I never spoke. I was afraid I would overshadow him. So I kept quiet. I played the role that was expected of me. I tried to be what other people wanted me to be, rather than what *I* wanted to be."

In terms of numbers second marriages seem to win the race for happiness, but they also score higher in the quality section, too. If one can compare degrees of happiness, or kinds of happiness, second marriages seem to inspire a higher quality, a more penetrating and serious relationship.

"It's a different sort of happiness now," a woman told me, "less innocent, more profound, less carefree, more wise. Perhaps on the happiness scale they are equal, my first and second marriages, but where quality is measured, the second marriage seems to have won."

It may, in fact, take more serious and important things to make one happier as one grows older. I can remember being exquisitely happy with a new dress, or delighting in a shocking prank. (I once walked out on a dinner party I was giving but not enjoying, went to the movies and left the guests to do the dishes.) Clothes don't thrill me so much now, that prank would not amuse me—even the thought embarrasses me, and I would not do it. Today, I am made happy by less expensive and dramatic but more important things, such as my son getting an A on a paper we all sweated over, my husband's noticing a chill in the air before I do and getting me a sweater, discovering that a friend shares the same opinion about something, or seeing a particularly beautiful display of daffodils that I broke my back planting the autumn before.

One person explained in simple terms what such happiness is like. "We have a new kind of intimate relationship, a more sexual one than either of us had before, and more deeply intellectual. I think one reason it is so very happy is that it is a total commitment to each other, which for some reason I never had dared to make before. There is unbelievable happiness."

Super Sex

Happiness is a general overall sensation made up of many different elements, and surely one of the most basic of these in any marriage is sex. A couple who does not enjoy compatible, harmonious sex, whether practiced often or not, simply can't have a very happy marriage. Although comparisons are difficult, most remarried people seem to feel that sex during the second marriage is much better, an important part of their total sense of exuberance. Suddenly, they are reborn—young, beautiful, important, on top of everything. The men and women I interviewed were unanimously positive about the importance of sex in their new lives. Sex the second time around was a devastatingly delightful experience, an incomparably thrilling emotion, a revitalization of all the senses that make life so pleasurable.

And there is even documented evidence that sex the second time is better. A love life can be measured on an unromantic scale called coital frequency, which refers to the number of times a month that couples have intercourse. Presumably, the sexier the marriage, or the more satisfying the sex, the more often the couple will find time to enjoy sex. According to the 1970 National Fertility Study,* for women who are married once for less than five years and are under twenty-five years of age, the coital frequency is ten times a month. In this same age group, for women who are in their second marriage and who have also been married less than five years, the coital frequency is eleven. (The reason for measuring frequency for marriages of less than five years' duration is that after a marriage has gone on for many years, the coital frequency will fall somewhat and it would be wrong to measure a second marriage of five years with a first marriage of twenty-five, or the other way around.) For women who are aged twenty-five to twenty-nine, coital frequency in a first marriage of less than five years was nine; for the same group in a second marriage the frequency was an average of ten. In every case, for women who had been married a short length of time, women in their second marriages were having sex more often than women in their first marriages.

One sees this sexual revitalization among older women even more sharply. For example, the thirty-five- to thirty-nine-year-old woman who is still in her first marriage has intercourse on the average of seven times a month, while her counterpart among remarried women of thirty-five to thirty-nine is having intercourse ten times.

Averages are of course merely middle points on the scale. A remarried friend of mine experienced such an extraordinary sexual appetite that he and his new wife had intercourse at least twenty-five times a month for many months. Like him, most people willingly told me

*Special tabulations from the 1970 National Fertility Study. See C. F. Westoff and N. B. Ryder, *The Contraceptive Revolution* (Princeton: Princeton University Press, 1976).

their intimate feelings about the importance of a new sex life in their second marriages. As one of them put it: "I never experienced these sex feelings before. They are more intense, there's more attraction. It is an astounding kind of thing."

For many of those I interviewed, having sex in a first marriage was difficult because of the lack of any kind of intelligent preparation. Without an understanding of human sexuality, of how to treat each other's sexual needs, people were not able to find satisfactory sex lives. Men and women need sex in different amounts and in different ways, and many had trouble in their first marriages communicating those needs to each other. It was all terribly embarrassing, and, like their parents, they didn't talk about it. Ways of satisfying each other had to be found by trial and error, and often were never really found.

"I have a much better sex life now," a woman said. "I'm more mature, more aware of myself. I hadn't learned to enjoy sex at nineteen. I was a traditional, uptight person and this inhibited me. In my first marriage, it was years before I had an orgasm, but I didn't even know I hadn't been having one. I felt something was wrong. I started reading books and then I realized."

"I hadn't had a sex life since my last child was born," a man told me. "I buried myself in work. Now, all of a sudden, life started up again. The second time it's a beautiful, easy relationship."

In talking about her sex life, a woman said she thought her first husband was impotent. Without really knowing what to expect, some women, apparently, live with whatever sex is offered by their husbands, who may have had slightly more experience than they have but probably know as little about the intricacies of sexual behavior as their wives do.

Part of the reason for sexual success in a remarriage may be that the couple wants love, sex, and a new secure life acutely at a time in their lives when they have been out of the mainstream. They want back in badly. After having had no sex at the time of divorce, and after experimenting with sex but without love, they are very receptive. Another part of the reason is that people usually live together before remarriage and can test their sexual compatibility, whereas most did not live with their first spouses before marriage. And, furthermore, it's the second time for one or both partners, and those who have been through marriage are likely to be more sexually skilled.

Of course, the sexual revolution of the 1970s, which left society feeling much more permissive about premarital and extramarital sex, has meant that lots of people are living together in and out of wedlock and talking about it more. Despite all the action and the talk, many people are still not very sexually sophisticated before marriage, many do not believe in relations with other men once they are married, and many have only an occasional fling of short duration. In a study* done by Dr. Melvin Zelnick and Dr. John F. Kantner of Johns Hopkins University in 1971, 5000 girls aged fifteen to nineteen were interviewed. The study showed that only a little more than 25 per cent of all never-married teen-age girls reported having had sexual intercourse. Seventy-five per cent of the girls had never had sexual intercourse, which may be quite a revelation to those who believe that by the 1970s virtually every kid who could make love was making love. Furthermore, although the frequency of intercourse varied with age, the majority of girls had intercourse less than three times a month. And because young people have not been promiscuous, more than half the girls had never had intercourse with more than one person after the time they began having sexual relations. According to Dr. Zelnick, there was obviously less sex in 1971 than a good many anxious adults thought there was. I imagine the amount of sexual activity and experimentation has increased somewhat between 1971 and today, but not enough to change any conclusions.

As far as extramarital sex is concerned, a 1975 survey of their readers by *Redbook* magazine showed that 30 per cent of those who completed the questionnaire had had sex outside of marriage. However, as the magazine itself pointed out, their sample of women was very lopsided, as it included only *Redbook* readers, most of whom were young. The fact that they voluntarily took part in the survey would also indicate a more positive sexual attitude than perhaps the average person might have. And some may have been having sex while still married but separated. Thus, taking a guess, the national average of married women who are sexually active with other men as well as their husbands would probably be something like only 10 per cent. So it would seem that our sexual experience before and outside of marriage is still spotty and does not by any means include the

*Melvin Zelnick and John F. Kantner, "Sexual Experience of Young Unmarried Women in the United States," *Family Planning Perspectives,* Vol. 4, No. 4, October 1972.

majority of women—attitudes may have changed more than actual practice has. The experience gained in a first marriage is still rather important and unique and heavily influences how people behave on the physical level in a second marriage.

For example, because of their familiarity with sex, remarried people are far more willing to divulge their sexual fantasies, which in the past, and often in first marriages, people were more likely to keep secret. A woman I know enjoyed being tied down to the bed during intercourse, and it wasn't until she experienced the relaxed relationship in her second marriage that she dared tell her husband. She was afraid she would be laughed at, but he didn't laugh, and was happy to oblige her. Sharing fantasies ought to be part of sexual compatibility. Men have often ignored this part of sex, thinking of women as passive, soft receptacles who are there just for them. Even the language and demonstrations of sex are no longer vulgar.

"I'm no longer embarrassed by sex," a woman told me. "We can openly enjoy each other's bodies without hiding them. We can talk about our sexual fantasies, even if they may seem a bit personal or odd. Everybody has them, and being able to bring them out in the open makes sex more interesting."

Another woman frankly complained that men in a first marriage don't, in her opinion, have enough sexual experience: "It's not just the orgasm," she said. "They don't know how to deal with a woman, how to really arouse her, like giving her an oral orgasm."

Men also found the difference noticeable. Said one: "I find my second marriage sexier. It's true that nothing compares with the first sex. But it's also true that nothing compares with two experienced lovers knowing how to satisfy each other."

"After some years of marriage," a woman admitted, "the sex starts going downhill. And to be able to start it again . . . the hunger and appetite of youth with the experience of years of practice, can be unbearably exciting. Not more exciting in the sense that it is new. But more exciting in the sense that it is more complicated, more unexpected, more varied."

One man remarked about how his second wife was less inhibited and even loved to walk nude around the apartment. He couldn't recall ever having seen his first wife do this; in fact, he couldn't remember ever having seen all of her in the nude at one time. Another man was equally enthusiastic: "The second time I felt great. Tremendous. It's a great experience. It's an exhilarating thing in mid-life. I was afraid I wouldn't know what to do, but instinct tells you. You're right back."

Certainly, part of the growing up that occurs before marriage should include some kind of sexual education, an understanding of the sexual needs of the male and female, how the human body works and what it looks like. Sex should be talked about in the home and taught in every school. Too many education systems fail to have mandatory courses which go beyond the most elementary facts. Experience tells us that the subject should be a natural one, not fraught with psychological hang-ups that are transmitted like some dread disease from parents to children, embellished by a lot of anxiety and misinformation picked up along the way. Without all this, the education has to take place the hard way.

Openness without End

Along with a greater sexual naturalness, people in a second marriage all remarked on the candidness and honesty with which they viewed all aspects of their entire relationship with their spouses. There were fewer areas of awkwardness. There were fewer moments when they had to suppress their real feelings to avoid causing pain—real or imagined—for themselves or their mates. Where the lines of communication are down, couples are unable to sustain an intimate relationship; but in second marriages, people seem able to talk about more things; they know each other better; they enjoy spending time with each other more; they get more out of living with each other. Both of them have survived the trauma of divorce and can come together with a common bond of experience. Even when only one member of the couple has been married and divorced, or when one is widowed and the other divorced, the situation is quite different than when it's the first time for both. It's easier to meet on open ground, share needs, hurts, and hopes, and establish an atmosphere of easy communication —which usually lasts. Those I spoke to described this openness as an important part of their remarriage (and it should be part of any relationship where people live with each other). Their comments about this heightened degree of communication could be taken as excellent advice to follow in establishing rapport with another person.

One woman described how it works for her: "If we fight, I'm a much better fighter now, more verbal. I don't withdraw as much. I'm more direct. If you can talk about a problem, you can resolve it. I came to believe I was a worthwhile person."

"We don't need to avoid topics," a man reported. "We can talk about anything society throws at us . . . mastectomy, retarded kids, remarriage, anything. We are open to having discussions about ideas people couldn't talk about before."

Instead of keeping everything pent up inside and feeling resentment, remarried people have learned to let it come out. But not in anger. They know by now that blind anger is stupid. "Now I'm more conscious of the things I can do to make my marriage better," a very attractive woman explained to me. "If something's wrong, we talk it out. I tell him, 'I know you don't like it, but I can't change and I don't want to change. I don't feel I have to change. I don't expect either of us to.' And so we just have to compromise. For example, the toilet paper. My husband always puts the toilet paper in the holder backward. I snap it in the other way. I live with the way he does it. I concede and I do so openly. But if I can't make the concession, I'll say so. In my first marriage I wouldn't say anything. I'd just resent it."

People told me they thought the most important thing in their relationship was to feel good about themselves, to be able to feel vulnerable, to be able to afford to cry or make a mistake, and not always to feel defensive. As one person put it: "We don't play games."

Remarriage doesn't overwhelm people the way marriage originally did. People don't usually compete with each other, but are more apt to take pride in each other's accomplishments, to enjoy each other rather than to feel jealousy about what the other person does. They also are not so desperate to hold on to marriage that they allow themselves to be taken advantage of. A woman who had been married three times said she no longer feared her husband or was intimidated by him: "I used to be afraid of fights because he was the only man I had and I didn't want to lose him. Now I am my own self. A person. The divorce and living alone made me a person. And it's a power I now have. I don't faint with joy because my husband chose to marry me. We chose each other this time and we each expect to remain an individual. He's just as afraid of losing me as I am of losing him. Which is hardly at all."

In a letter I received from a man, he described a similar experience of finding a new freedom in remarriage: "My genes tend to make me volcanic and dramatic, so the development of our relationship hasn't been quite as calm as glass. But the great thing about it is that there is no feeling or response that we can't talk about or manage. In my twenty years of first marriage I meandered through innumerable swamps of inchoate feelings, compulsions, and rigidities and suffered the despair of knowing that things were out of control, going bad, and not knowing why, and not being able to say anything meaningful about it all. So that the present skills I enjoy with the woman I love, in dealing with feelings, angers, jealousies, wants, in being able to identify and handle what's going on between us, is a great privilege indeed. It's a very strong thing to share this common language, common theory of behavior, and common method for handling distress."

Realistic Expectations

Happiness comes in part from knowing what you want, from wanting something attainable and then attaining it. Henry Kissinger once made a remark about history that could also serve as an apt description of an unsuccessful marriage: "History is a tale of efforts that failed, or aspirations that weren't realized, or wishes that were fulfilled and then turned out to be different from what one expected." A striking characteristic of remarriage is that most people involved in one have pretty realistic expectations of what they can demand of a marriage and of another person. Understanding what marriage is all about in practical terms, knowing what it can offer and what can be asked of it, and what one's partner can and cannot give, make disappointment and failure less apt to happen. Each partner is far more likely to be able to capitalize on what the marriage does offer and not yearn for some impossible, unrealistic situation that can never exist.

"The first time I had all those expectations," a woman remembered, "What my husband should have been, what life should have been. I bought the whole package. When it didn't turn out that way, I was disillusioned. I love my life now, but I'm envious that others can live for sixty years with one husband and I can't have that."

"The second time you don't look for perfection," someone else commented. "It's not smooth or sunny all the time. We both knew that the euphoria of the first six months couldn't last. We knew we'd have some problems. The first time you think you'll be high all the time."

Several women mentioned that the first time they married they thought they would have the "being-in-love-forever" feeling always, and when they had to clean the toilets or whatever, it kind of ruined things for them. One woman cheerfully admitted that her second husband is not perfect, but she also realized that she wasn't perfect either, nor was anyone else. When one expects the person, the sex, the love, and the relationship to be perfect in an unreal sense, one is almost certain to have the bottom of the marriage drop out at some point. A man said quite briefly: "I have a hell of a lot fewer illusions about what sort of work it takes. But it's work that I enjoy."

Having real expectations about marriage means that one has grown into this understanding. You're certainly not born with it. One remarried woman assured me that she and her husband knew enough about each other "to give an honest picture of me to him and him to me. We didn't have to put up a false image of ourselves. When you're young there's not that much to know. The first time you establish a pattern, you pretend you are what you aren't. Once you are committed to become that way, it's difficult to change. We ended up living in a way we didn't like. We disliked ourselves but there was nothing we could do."

Greater Tolerance

One of the benefits of greater openness and understanding in remarriage is the gentle tolerance with which a couple has learned to treat each other. They tend to be far more considerate of each other's feelings than they ever were before. A doctor told me: "I may be getting older, but I'm more tolerant. I'm really happy, so little things don't bother me so much. And you certainly want to make it work. I don't see how I could face another failure. It's a searing experience to break up a marriage. It doesn't help your sense of your own worth. Thank God you have a second chance, and this one has got to work."

Other people said that minor irritations didn't bother them and that it was important to remember that the other person is a human being too. Because they had lived in that strange realm of middle-aged singlehood after a first marriage, they knew what it meant to come home late or tired, to burn the chicken, to fail to make the bed, and they could be far more tolerant if their partner was guilty of the same thing. They were no longer so tense about perfection. A woman told me that soon after she met the man who later became her second husband, they were riding in a car and he was forced to stop short. As he did so, he grabbed her with his outstretched arm and said, "Careful, don't hit your head." She was absolutely astounded with his concern. No one she had ever known, and certainly not her first husband, had ever worried about whether she banged her head or not. In her first marriage her husband took care of himself and she took care of him, and no one took care of her. Her second marriage to this man continued on the same note of mutual consideration on which it had begun.

A man told me his second wife had some habits that bothered him and that would certainly have gotten on his nerves in his first marriage. But he realized that he had some annoying traits too—continually leaving the toothpaste cap off the tube, constantly blocking the television screen with a knee or foot as they watched it in bed. Recognizing his own faults had made him far more tolerant of hers, and their annoyances canceled each other out, eventually becoming unimportant.

This effort at being sympathetic has been observed by others. In a conversation I had with Dr. Wardell B. Pomeroy, a New York marriage counselor, he said he also found a greater capacity for tolerance in people in their second marriages, even those he saw who were having problems. Not only do people learn to accept others' failures by recognizing their own but, having lost everything, they are far more careful the second time not to make stupid mistakes about unimportant things. Their new relationships are too crucial to waste emotions on which way the toilet paper is fitted into the holder. They are more likely to do what they *don't* feel like doing, because it seems to mean a lot to their partner and doesn't matter so much to them. They now look at life together with different priorities and sets of values.

The Role of Women's Liberation

The loosening up of divorce laws and the women's liberation movement have certainly played a strong role in changing the character of women's response to marriage. And this new response has put new pressures upon marriage, pressures that may be difficult for some men to meet. But when the spouses are aware of the woman's desire to play an equal part in the marriage, it has given that marriage an added strength and excitement. Regardless of the official position the partners may or may not take on women's lib, there is a certain amount of liberated independence that remarrying people bring with them, something which became part of them during that murky period of finding themselves. There is also the new experience of housekeeping, which the man between marriages learns to accept, and the woman between marriages learns to minimize, and it is not likely that anyone who remarries will slip into the role of slave driver, slave, king, or consort. It is much more probable that the marriage will begin with a flavor of equality, whether stated or not, and this is one of the more important benefits a remarriage offers. Women's lib has helped to make this kind of free-flowing relationship more respectable—if not actually fashionable. If he does the laundry and she takes the car in to the mechanic, they each feel that they are expanding the universe that marriage encompasses, and thus their own.

One man remarked that remarriage for him was different because after he was divorced he got used to cleaning and cooking. "I was damned if I was going to eat frozen food. Then when I remarried, with my wife working, I had to help. She got the lawn, and I did the garden beds, which I liked. I bathed the kids, which she didn't like to do. I felt strongly that I have to help with cleaning or cooking or whatever is needed. I do it. We don't do sex role-playing. We do what needs to be done."

A woman told me pretty much the same story. She said her husband helps much more around the house than most men: "We split the work and there were no expectations that it would be any different. We don't artificially divide it up. We both cook. We both clean up. We both do the dishes."

This sounds like the perfect formula for a successful marriage, and for most couples who remarry, it has become the only way to live. Obviously it can work in a first marriage too, if the couple is lucky and has given their relationship a lot of thought, and the man is flexible and willing. But let's face it: so far, women are much more interested in women's lib than men are, and it usually takes a shock like divorce to awaken male interest in an equal arrangement. Men in first marriages are slowly beginning to change, or at least make a gesture, perhaps because they want to stay young and with it. A rather conservative middle-aged man I know, whose devoted wife will do anything for him, suddenly insisted on doing the dinner dishes. His wife's incredulous explanation: "It's women's lib!"

Besides its effect on housework, the women's movement has opened thousands of locked doors inside thousands of women's minds. They have realized, almost in unison, that they aren't crazy to want a different kind of life. There has been a public acceptance of a new role in marriage for women. All those people who had quietly stifled tears and resentments and aspirations were now free to express these emotions to the men they lived with. Most remarriages that began in the 1970s were deeply influenced by this new freedom and incorporated it into their own relationships from the beginning. As one woman put it: "Women's lib legitimized my feelings. It's easier now to express my needs to someone else. We have less stereotyped roles." And a man put it this way: "In my second marriage we have more respect for each other. Women's lib meant there were lots of women going to law school or to work, and husbands were shedding the old ideas and being proud of their little housewives." Any kind of equality or mutual self-respect is a big plus for any marriage. The partners are certain to get along better than where there is a hierarchy.

In addition to the fact that much more thought and discussion go into the decision about whether the marriage is a good and workable idea, the two partners enter the union with a lot of "givens." Discussions may be romantic, but they will also resemble in some ways a business deal among equals. How much money, children, furniture is he/she contributing and how much am I? It's very much like the merger of two independent companies and their assets. This coming together on the same footing usually continues well into the marriage, deepening the bonds of equality and equal respect, which many first marriages, founded more haphazardly, never find. The woman who thinks that a "total woman" is a female whose role in life is solely that of titillating her husband—meeting him at the door every evening dressed in the suggestive finery of an aging, rather desperate prostitute who is trying to arouse an aging, rather desperate man—and obeying his every command is just kidding herself. Men can buy those services easily enough, but companionship founded on a base of love, respect, and sharing in equal proportions has no price and lasts a lot longer.

The realization that you are two equals involved in the successful, ongoing business of a profitable life is very rewarding and stimulating. One man told me about the change remarriage had made in his life, describing how they made decisions together: "It was never a subject of discussion before. My new wife and I now make decisions taking into account two equal people with careers which are equally important. Everything used to be my decision. There was no teamwork, no effort at compromise. Now we talk about both our feelings instead of hiding them."

A Sharing of Interests

As we have seen, all the strands that work for a happy marriage are interrelated. Experience has made people more tolerant and open-minded, more willing to consider new and revised ways of thinking —such as women's rights to greater freedom and equality—which lead to further openness and tolerance. Another beneficial side effect is that remarrying couples tend to enjoy a sharing of interests that usually does not exist in first marriages, and to find themselves more open to new interests and new people. Through the new partner, one finds scores of ready-made friends anxious to make one feel wanted. One develops tastes and activities never before dreamed of. A sedentary wife becomes a whirlwind on the tennis court; a portly husband sheds pounds while munching his new wife's natural-food dinners. He discovers he really likes opera, and she reads her first novel in years and actually enjoys it. A lot of dormant interests come alive, a lot of new ones take root and flower.

A tennis-playing friend admitted: "I couldn't play tennis with my previous husband. We'd lose a point and he'd almost throw the racquet at me. Now I love tennis. My new partner is very different from my first husband. He is more in tune with me. He reinforces what feels good."

In a number of first marriages that I've observed, husbands and wives don't share an interest in each other's work. The husband often doesn't seem to care what his wife does all day so long as dinner is ready when he gets home, and she is very likely not to know or understand a great deal about the intricacies of his work, except for his salary check. A friend of mine who has college-age sons was surprised recently when they asked him if he would mind telling them what it was he really did all day long. He had never bothered to explain any more than what they already knew—that he was in the steel business—and no one had ever thought of asking. Many men find the knotty details of their business too complex to describe to their wives, who, they feel, wouldn't be interested anyway. In a remarriage, it is far more likely that the man and woman will take an active interest in each other's work, often getting valuable advice from the other or sharing the same career. It's all the result of a more total and planned union than they had before, of getting to learn about each other after the careers are fully formed, and of a deeper caring about the other person.

I was deluged with positive comments: "My life has changed so drastically. We have an awful lot of fun together. He doesn't like me to do things without him, and that's kind of nice." "I'm interested in my husband's work for the first time. I'm more intellectually stimulated. We do more things together."

A woman I know became interested in architecture because she married an architect, and they spend vacations touring around Europe delighting in finding old buildings and art deco furniture. A man (in fact, many men) remarked that their second wives are more involved in their work, and often go on business trips with them. The sharing of more things leads to a greater appreciation of each other and makes marriage a more intense experience. While looking for another mate these people probably realized that they wanted someone they could have better communication with than they had with their previous partner. It would appear, from what people say, that to have a good marriage you need to have common interests and even share some of the same habits and compulsions. One man told me he deliberately chose a second wife whose ideas fitted with his, and to him this made his wife far more interesting.

In a late marriage it is much easier to assess someone's interests and decide how they fit in with yours. Whether he or she rates high not only in sexual compatibility but in mental rapport. How satisfying it will be to live and work with that person. Whether she can really care if he gets that ad account, or he gives a damn about whether she is asked to catalogue the paintings. Being able to care about the other person's interests and work enables one to be in love on more planes of consciousness. More parts of you are in love with more parts of him or her. You touch in more places. There are simply more common feelings when interests coincide and can be shared.

A Sense of Humor and Awareness

A sense of humor is a rare and precious quality which remains undeveloped in many people until they reach a kind of self-awareness and self-confidence that allows them to laugh at themselves and at things around them. Some never do reach this point. Curiously—or perhaps not so curiously—remarried couples often mention that the sense of humor which they share with each other is one of the basic ingredients in their happy remarriages. One man said almost proudly: "Either one can make the other laugh in two seconds. We have great rapport. Our thinking is fine-tuned." And another told me that he and his wife shared what he called "a sense of the ridiculous" and could always laugh at what looked like a serious problem.

Awareness—of which humor is an extension—is also a vital component of what makes marriage work. So often in a bad marriage a person's frustrations can go totally unrecognized simply because he isn't aware of her fatigue, her boredom, her need for change or variety, or she isn't aware of his desire for more frequent sex, more interesting meals, his feelings of fatigue or boredom, his need for understanding and sympathy. Most remarried couples seem to have a sharpened sensitivity to the other person's moods, probably because each one's sensory antennae have been heightened by marital disaster. They react to the slightest nuances. It doesn't take a hammer blow to turn them on and start them vibrating. So many times a man would say, "I'm more aware of my wife and what she's like and what I'm like. My first relationship was pretty automatic."

People Try Harder

This heightened awareness, this internal radar that is constantly awake and scanning, means not only that couples are familiar with what it takes to make their marriage work but that they actually try harder to make the marriage succeed. Dr. Harold I. Lief, director of the Marriage Council of Philadelphia, confirmed my findings about this intense desire for success: "Couples in their second marriage who come to me show great concern about whether they're going to make it. They work hard. They're more tuned in to the nature of the relationship, and they find it easier to deal with their sexual problems." Mrs. Belle Parmet, the psychiatric social worker who has been counseling couples for thirty years concurs: "The remarried people I see have a different attitude. They are often committed to work things out. Compared with those in a first marriage, they seem to take more time examining the problems and are able to talk more openly about them."

Nearly everyone I spoke to said that he or she worked harder to make their second marriage a success than they ever had in a first marriage. Perhaps having made a better choice of mate the second time, any extra effort they put in pays off more readily when problems do appear. Perhaps also, even though they would divorce more easily if things were not good, they do not look forward to yet a third try and would like to see the second one be *it.* They have some experience to draw on, and know what a shambles these mid-life switches can be.

"I try harder to make this marriage work," a woman explained. "I avoid foolishly irritating my husband. I try not to be selfish, to see his point of view. I'm willing to compromise. Winning every argument, getting my way, is no longer important. We are considerate of each other."

Another woman said she knew there were good and bad things in any marriage and that in her second one she tried to concentrate on the good. A man said he tried to avoid arguments, "but you don't have to try as hard because certain things are not as important, such as which way the toothpaste is squeezed, how the shirts are done, who cooks dinner."

With everyone making such a concerned effort, giving it all they've got, and with all the inherent rewards and benefits of remarriage, with people declaring they are far happier the second time, it seems that despite the incredible problems of children, money, and ex-spouses, remarriage is one kind of marriage worth having.

There is, however, one more point to be made. I don't think remarriage as we know it could have existed in an earlier time or in a vacuum. I don't think people who have praised remarriage so highly could have taken full advantage of it without the help of the current social atmosphere, nor could they have taken advantage of the opportunities the environment offers quite so readily without a first marriage in their backgrounds. Remarriage seems to be a phenomenon whose time has come. Not only is it the major alternative to remaining divorced, to a bad marriage, or to giving up married life, but both remarriage and society in general share strong interests that have come alive in the 1970s: caring about others, honesty, personal happiness and fulfillment, the freedom to be one's self, a new sexual freedom, the desire to elevate women to equal status, and to look upon war (perhaps even personal wars) with horror.

Much of what couples bring to remarriage is a result of what they see changing around them. Beginning again, they are able to adopt it in their own personal platform. They are influenced by the new codes and concerns of the very young; they are affected by the media passion for women's lib and consciousness-raising; they are influenced by the current interest in psychiatric counseling. And who among us can remain oblivious to the shelves bursting with "advice" books on divorce and how to solve marital hang-ups creatively, or the magazines which give monthly statistics on how many are having extramarital affairs and why, discuss the desire for more sex among women, and give advice on how to live in an open marriage where anything goes. It is obviously a time of exposure, talking about our ills, talking about the cures, talking about marital problems, sexual problems, career problems, women's problems, and pondering men's problems—the mid-life switches in career, and how to stay home and housekeep and mind the babies while wives go to work. There is no one whose consciousness has not been agitated on all levels. It is the kind of atmosphere in which our mass second marriages are flourishing. Both this general air of liberation from the past and from their own first marriage experiences have benefited couples trying it for a second time.

THE
FUTURE
OF MARRIAGE

7

I once read a book that referred to marriage as restrictive, possessive, and monotonous. The motivations for marrying that once existed—sex, economic security, and babies—no longer pertain to the same extent. Sex, security, and—to a lesser degree—babies can be enjoyed without a legal marriage. There is more illegitimacy among the single and more adultery among the married these days. Some people say that traditional marriage smothers their individuality, is too constricting, and doesn't leave room for enough sexual adventure. More than half of all existing marriages are probably not happy ones but only legally stamped unions that limp along. Marriage does not always seem to be the answer to the way we ought to live together. Yet by middle age, all but 4 per cent of American women are married, as are all but 5 per cent of American men. As we know, it doesn't always work. In 1975, there were 2.5 million men and 4 million women in the United States who reported their marital status as divorced at the time the Census sample survey was taken. More than 2 million of these people were divorced in 1975 alone.

Is Marriage Dead?

All around me there is marital turbulence. My editor has just remarried; an editor in the same firm has just separated from his wife; one of my doctors has left home and rented an apartment for himself and his mistress, leaving his wife with a flock of children to raise; one of my best friends is having an affair which his wife knows about; and another good friend is on the verge of divorce. My neighbor on the right is remarried, and the one on my left is also remarried.

At least first marriage, in the form in which we know it, does not look as though it is flourishing. We may be witnessing a dying institution. I am not suggesting remarriage as a cure-all for our marriage problems. I'd rather see people learn enough to avoid problems before any marriage. Not all remarriages make it, of course. And not everyone who wants to remarry can find someone. But remarriage seems to be the answer for many who are unhappily married, those who are divorced and who want to be married, and those who never imagined that one marriage could last them all their lives. It is the answer for people who made mistakes and want another chance, for people who thought they were getting one thing and found themselves getting something else and living a totally different kind of life they can't adjust to. It is right for people who have grown in different ways or at different speeds and are no longer compatible. It may work for people whose first partners were neurotic, alcoholic, or too demanding. It is full of opportunity for people who change their minds about what they want out of life, people who suddenly know what they really want to do. It's the answer for those whose husbands or wives walk out on them, those hurt and maimed people who did not sense the need for divorce at the same time that their partners did. Remarriage is the big chance for happiness for those who still want marriage but haven't found it with the right person. It may well be the cure-all for many divorced people now in the single state, and the millions of couples who are married but not really enjoying it.

People have found the rules of traditional marriage very confining, particularly when they are young, looking ahead to a full lifetime of partnership. It is unrealistic to expect marriage always to work, always to be interesting, always to stay fresh and alive and capable of growth. It necessarily grows stale as the people within it change or grow bored with each other and their routine. And that is when they ought to make a switch. We have in large part gotten over the hang-up that divorce is wrong—but not completely. People still tend to see divorce as a washout of some kind. Divorce, as I have said, need not be synonymous with lack of success. It can be a sign that one is moving on to the next phase. It is not necessary to wait until the two members of the marriage are ready to kill each other before they conclude the partnership; the time to recast one's life can be felt much sooner than that. It is true that divorce is often a tragic thing when one member of the couple wants to move on and the other one does not, but it is a risk people take. If one or both people feel they are no longer really happy and the relationship cannot be improved, they *should* move on. As one remarried woman phrased her attitude: "I don't think of marriage as forever. If marriage is going to be for forty or fifty years, no. At twenty-one you don't have a clue to what you will be. Change is good and healthy. Relationships need work. Go in with a commitment that it will be forever, but knowing that it may not be." The fact that people live longer may be the reason for some divorce, but it's far from the whole story. Divorce is becoming increasingly popular among the very young.

People can no longer depend on one marriage, or one man or one woman as their very own, forever. There is no forever. Once we recognize all the millions of divorces as a symptom of the need to change, society will be ready to redefine marriage, to reexamine and restructure it to fit the specifications of modern men and women. Marriage must be understood in different terms, so that, when it ends, men will stop feeling guilty about hurting women and children unnecessarily because they will no longer be made to feel at fault. And women must learn never to live for only one man and one marriage. If the one man and the one marriage works for them, then, bravo! But there are too many for whom it doesn't work. In reviewing my notes on the histories of remarried men and women, I have at moments almost been moved to angry tears at the rotten deal that some women have received as men wanted to and did leave the marriage. It is true that some domineering women deserve to be left and that some men have had a rocky time, but they are not in the majority.

An Appeal to Women

When a marriage turns sour, there are always two sides to the problem. As everyone knows who has watched close friends split up, it's difficult to assign blame. Nevertheless, given the economic dependency of many women, it seems to this observer that in a breakup, women are unfortunately the ones who most commonly take the beating. Thus, at the risk of sounding a strident feminist trumpet, which I don't intend, I would like at this point to appeal to women to think of their futures, right from the beginning, to think in terms of securing their *own* fates, their own economic independence, to arrange their lives with the same determination and planning as men do. If divorce does come they will not be destroyed, their souls and spirits will not be shattered; they too will be capable of deciding when they have had enough. They won't then let men walk all over them, begging the man to stay in the marriage, threatening to take an overdose of Seconal if he leaves, wondering how they will bring up children themselves, having no separate life of their own on which they can depend. Women must be strong enough to walk out, strong enough psychologically to leave when the marriage is no longer productive. A woman whose husband has left her must stop wondering what she did that was wrong and blaming herself for not being good enough, hoping that he will leave that other woman and come back to them. He won't.

I think marriage counselors who operate on the principle that their function is to try to keep marriages together are wrong. What they ought to do is talk about reality and help the people involved separate with some dignity. To work, marriage must be an equal relationship that involves respect and admiration. Once these are lost, no counselor can reconstruct a marriage. A counselor's most important functions should be to keep a man from botching up the job of separation and to elevate the woman's usually damaged self-esteem. Women have got to protect themselves from the possible demise of their coupleness, and to think of the possibility of remarriage as an exciting next step.

As a further appeal, I think it will eventually make a great difference if women think in terms of bringing their children up, both the boys and the girls, with equal values and a similar sense of responsibility toward others. Today the demands of marriage are rapidly changing, spurred along by feminism, and men are simply not prepared by their parents for these changes. The boy children that our women bear, and love to death, are in no way ready to understand these new meanings. No demands have ever been made upon them. They are used to asking and getting and taking. It is very likely that the manner in which women deal with their children today will help determine the number of divorces and successful marriages in the future.

For this reason, remarried men often seem to make better husbands than those who are married once. They have come to realize, the hard way, that marriage is not what mother brought them up to think it was. They have learned to live alone. They have learned to do things for themselves. They have certainly learned more about what caring for others means.

Mothers also can sometimes be influential as role models for what their sons expect in a wife. A man I talked to had serious doubts about his wife's working because his own mother had refused to work and had stayed home with the kids. Because of this, he now feels this is what a woman should do. What he doesn't realize is that this route may have left his mother an angry and frustrated person, something his wife has no intention of becoming. It will be hard for him to relearn what roles each member of the family is supposed to play. It's true that most mothers didn't work, but many mothers and wives now want to or need to. Women now make up nearly 40 per cent of the U.S. labor force. Almost half of all women over the age of sixteen in the country work, or to put it in more visible terms, 37 million women have jobs. Working couples have become more and more common and there will be more of them in the future. A remarried woman explained why it is so important for her to work: "I like to be independent. I have to be able to maintain my own financial identity. I fought hard to be financially independent. I'd never go back to being a housewife."

Any woman who enters marriage without constructing an independent life for herself—a job, friends, some money in the bank—is taking a chance these days. In the future more women will insist on having a marriage that includes a career for themselves, an independent bank account, an independent personality, and self-esteem. Future marriages sound as though they are going to be infinitely more interesting and much more fun than some of the childish episodes into which marriage has deteriorated. The recently divulged affairs involving Eisenhower, Roosevelt, Kennedy, and various congressmen make it more dramatically clear, if it wasn't already so, that people need more than they have been "allowed" to have, and that traditional marriage needs alternatives. Future marriage will offer many. There is no longer any point in being hypocritical about what challenges and stimulation and variety many people need, not only those at the top in Washington (and I don't mean just sex). It's time to snuff out the puritanical memory and stop kidding ourselves. Marriage will not often be permanent or monogamous. Our sixty-five to eighty years on this planet, however short a duration it really is, can offer a much more intense personal fulfillment than we ever have given it a chance to do before.

On Future Divorce

As divorce has become easier to obtain, people no longer have to stage fake adultery scenes in which prepaid photographers rush into prepaid hotel rooms to find one member of the unhappy couple in bed with a prepaid model. People are beginning to look upon divorce as part of life, something that will be seen and resorted to more often, something which in the future may be even simpler and more automatic to obtain. The pointless expense of getting a divorce is absurd. As one remarried woman said: "If our marriage doesn't make us happy, we won't continue. People have that in the back of their minds. But we should change the divorce laws. Make divorce less expensive with less chance for hostility." Several remarried women corroborated the way I think most people will react in the future:

"People will not think of marriage in the future as forever. They will just expect to grow in different directions. They will dissolve things amicably. It will be possible to look at each other and say, 'We'd be better off if we split.'"

"Having got up the courage to leave the first time, I don't look on divorce as such a big trauma. I see it as a real alternative."

Asking for a divorce in the future will not take so much courage, and women who will gradually develop more self-respect will not desperately try to hang on to sick marriages. There will certainly be more spirit and independence among women.

On Future Marriage

But what about marriage itself? What about people who have experienced an unhappy marriage? How do they feel about it? Many are still sold on the institution, but others are not so sure. What is obvious is that men and women are considering marriage in ways that never occurred to them before. They are examining it, criticizing it, doing all the groundwork that is necessary before the institution itself can be transformed. I think the remarried people of today are like the revolutionary cadres of some great political upheaval. This revolution in marriage styles may be more gradual and subtle than most revolutions, but compared with many other social changes, it seems to be rushing right along. Considering that marriage and the family has been the bulwark of American values for the entire life of this country, it is really amazing that it is only in the last five years that customs have been sharply altered.

Those Who Are for It

No one I talked to was willing to think of marriage as absolutely permanent, a trap, something you stayed with no matter what. But some still believe in the value and necessity of marriage as we now know it. The surprising thing was that the pros and cons stacked up about 50-50. There were many more people than I had suspected who were critical of marriage. Yet many still see it as essential in the future and rely on the importance of the marriage commitment. A woman pointed out: "Not getting married would not be an answer for me. There is something about publicly declaring that you are taking the responsibility and committing yourself to this person. Marriage is the best arrangement for me."

Another woman also expressed her belief in the importance of marriage. She said: "I see all the bad parts of people living together without marriage. I also see bad marriages. But I think the commitment you make is what makes it work."

In similar words another woman said: "Marriage is important. It's part of a commitment, a public avowal. People take it more seriously. Before people became so mobile, you knew a person's family very well when you married. You decided who you wanted after looking around. You thought this person was the best thing you could get. Now strangers marry. People don't have the opportunity to know each other before marriage. There are more problems, but it's still important."

Another woman thought it would be ideal if people could have just one marriage. And she was strongly in favor of the institution because "If you are just living together, it's too damn easy to leave. If not for the legal agreement, you wouldn't bother to work it out."

Most people who found marriage essential believe that people marry too young. "Marrying at eighteen is stupid. You are so young. You haven't lived enough. You don't know who you are and you make immature decisions. Little things that are important then are not important later on."

Another person commented: "Maybe people shouldn't get married until they are at least forty or older. You want experience when you are young, and companionship when you get old."

A woman told me she believed in marriage but would feel better if her children had three or four different experiences of living together, equivalent to three or four marriages before they actually married. "It ought to be as difficult to get married as it is to get divorced," she said.

There were other views as to why marriage is important: "I like being married," a woman admitted. "I feel more secure emotionally than I do living with someone. I can't give freely without the security of marriage."

People enjoy marriage because of the opportunity for tradition it affords. "I don't like the idea of shaking hands and saying good-by to go off and try a different life-style," a woman said. "Our shared experience is so important. It takes time to develop. Marriage needs time. I don't see doing lots of different things and living different ways in the future."

People also pointed to the importance of marriage for them when children are involved. "Experiment before having kids," a woman advised. "Kids need stability. You can't go in different directions constantly with kids. They can't take it. When you have children you must establish a secure situation."

"Marriage is necessary because there are these other people involved. Without it there is a lack of rites and rituals to give us security. The backbone is taken away without it," a woman explained, "and we flounder."

Another woman who is strongly in favor of marriage said rather appreciatively: "It's a wonderful thing that my once-married friends could adjust to the different stages of marriage. It's luck to be in the right place at the right time. To find someone who's going to work for you. I admire those who've made it."

Marriage for many, then, remains a strength-giving and wholesome context in which to live, though even they wish it could be more perfect.

Those Who Are against It

There are those who because of a number of new developments have decided that marriage as we now live it may not be the answer for people in the future. They have been influenced by one bad marriage that soured beyond redemption, by the new opportunities for women, by the whole philosophy of feminism, by changes in the family itself. With fewer children, more career opportunities, a more mobile existence, a longer life-span, and the disappearance of a host of rigidities, such as religious, social, and legal strictures about divorce and singleness and remarriage, there are many more options to choose from. With all these new possibilities open to people now—new styles that are free of shame or society's condemnation—some people are naturally not going to stay in the narrow paths that everyone once blindly followed. They are going to do more thinking about how they feel and what they want. Choice and variety can be quite wonderful, particularly for women who have been excluded from most of these opportunities for so long. But it's also true for men who, whatever option they choose, will make it free and clear from shame and guilt, much happier and more genuine.

A recent news report described a survey taken of almost ten thousand men and women in the Common Market countries of Europe. The question asked was: "Taking all things together, how would you say things are these days? Would you say you're very happy, pretty happy, or not too happy?" The largest percentage describing themselves as very happy, 23 per cent, were people living together but not married and the smallest were those married but separated. The unmarried who are living together seem to have found something a lot of the others haven't, though the report I read did not state how long each group had been living together.

American men and women who question the necessity for marriage have begun to make pointed efforts to think about and seek their own routes to adult happiness. Some feel that a legal marriage is not necessary. "It makes no difference at all," a man said. "It's just easier the way the world is set up with checking accounts, kids' last names, etc."

A woman remarked that "legal marriage is not necessary. I have friends who have lived together without marrying and their breakup can be just as traumatic and as bitter. It's more important to look at how the relationship is supposed to be. The law just gives you more to fight about."

Others found marriage too narrow a setup. Said a woman: "Marriage can be too confining, too limiting to one's personal growth. You want a fluid open experience with multiple involvements."

Another person found marriage limiting for sexual reasons: "We had passionate sex before we remarried. I think it was one of those beautiful relationships that was ruined by marriage. Our life-style changed. We settled into a more conventional existence, but the sex life is still better than my first marriage. Perhaps, though, we shouldn't have bothered to marry at all."

A man told me why he and the woman he lives with have not remarried. "My friend," he said, "is not at all sure she ever wants to marry again. She reports regular evidence of discord among married friends and acquaintances and believes that marriage carries with it such powerful, implicit straitjackets of mind and behavior that inevitably oppression and limitations of freedom result."

Others also want to hold on to whatever independence they have attained. A woman conjectured about the future of marriage: "I think there will be less marriage and remarriage as independent, professional women refuse to give up their independence."

Another woman who also values her independence as a separate person and doesn't want to give it up and remarry said: "The problem with being married is the hang-up of owning another person. Society thinks in terms of two instead of 'he' and 'she.' You are supposed to go where the other person goes. My friend and I don't want to own each other. But if we both remarried, it's what society would impose on us, living together in one place, being invited everywhere together. Sometimes I'd rather go out alone when I'm going to see people who bore him. You can be more open just living together, but the arrangement is not good when there are kids."

A number of people who have remarried feel that if a second marriage fails, it means they were not meant for marriage and simply won't try again. Said one: "If I made two bad judgments, it's not so good. Maybe as a way of life, I'd have to say, it's not the thing for me."

New possibilities have begun to intrigue even those who are happily remarried and who don't plan to ever leave their second marriages. They consider what alternatives they might have chosen which might have been more practical and had better results in avoiding an unhappy first marriage and a drawn-out divorce. One person suggested contract marriages which just lay out the guidelines and which can easily be renegotiated every few years or terminated fairly easily. Another person also suggested that short-term contracts might be best. One woman warned that she thought it took extremely mature people to have a strong tie to each other if they are not married, but she thought it would be a more rewarding relationship.

A Case History—Con

A remarried, slender, artistic woman who is a teacher and is married to a man in medical research sat on the floor in her tree-shaded living room and talked about the stress that marriage creates in her life. Sitting on the floor makes one feel nearer to reality and truth, and we both felt close and able to communicate. She said that she was happier in her second marriage and then she explained what problems marriage held for her. I simply let her ramble on, in her case against marriage.

"My second marriage is far better than my first. But the second one is not perfect either. There are problems. I've changed and he hasn't.

He doesn't want me to change. I didn't really want to marry the second time. I had in mind an idyllic relationship, an exchange. But he wanted to marry and swept me into it. If I ever end this marriage, I would like to live alone.

"I know what I want, but I always have to compromise and try to please the man I live with. I'm always asked to see myself as crazy, or neurotic, or sick, while the man is always fine. The man never says, 'I'm depressed. I can't cope. I feel bad,' or even thinks these things. My attempts at openness are misunderstood. Men always see themselves as 'all together.' If something's wrong, it obviously can't be their fault.

"My second husband is a good companion, but he'll never rest till I become what he wants . . . a superwoman. Take care of his kids, work, give dinner parties, get a Ph.D., be sexually fantastic, be beautiful.

"And sex. He is very demanding. After I had more experience I realized something was lacking in his sexual aggression. It's sometimes frightening, overwhelming. He makes me feel like an object, a non-person. A finger up here. A tweak there. I am not as interested in sex as he is. He's resentful and troubled that I appear to lack all this sex drive. He doesn't even satisfy me. I don't have an orgasm. He's hardly ever given me one. I can't tell him. It's too embarrassing. He would think less of me. It bothers him that I'm not turned on sexually when he wants it, but it also pleases him because he thinks I'm safe. I won't play around. I miss a good sex life.

"I don't really like marriage because I have a sense that my needs are unimportant. He asks me to do things that are impossible. I don't make these demands of him. Sometimes I get this threatened feeling that he's trying to destroy me. At times he gets very angry. But I don't have to drink alcohol or take Valium. I don't need his understanding. He'll have to handle his own anger. But I turn his anger inward. There's no letup in his pressure to do things.

"I feel that I can take care of myself. I feel independent. And he resents it. So if I can take care of myself, I don't need him and all the problems with him. I do like to be with him, though, and in the good times we have a good relationship. But my life alone seems more attractive to me. If I were alone and I felt like going out, I would. If

A Case History—Con   153

not, I wouldn't. I'd feel free. Do you know what that is? That breath of freedom?"

Her long-haired cat walked through the room and she watched him disappear before she continued:

"I think divorce is a sign of health. People are able to take steps, to do something. But I don't want to put myself in the marriage market or the sex market. I don't see myself the way a man sees me. I don't want to be reflected in a man's eyes. Women today behave as though they are socially constructed to reinforce a man's ego and importance. We see marriage unrealistically. There is no understanding of human relationships. We are only concerned with the certificate. Whether we marry or not is unimportant, unless we want property, or our kids to be legitimate.

"My second marriage is better than my first. Maybe my third would be even better. I've learned a lot. Been forced to learn. I had to talk to a psychiatrist. I couldn't put it together myself. I suppose one long marriage is possible, but not likely.

"I see life in a sequential way. To see a marriage that ends as a failure is just flagellating yourself. I also think men expect too much service from a woman, and women might quite often be happier without men. Another thing, I would also like to get to know women better. I've never had serious women friends. I think women may be more interesting than men are."

A Case History—Pro

I met this rather trim remarried woman in her office. Cobwebs of green plants hung from hooks, and books on corporate law filled the shelves. She is important, has a good job, a husband who also has an excellent job, and two children. A housekeeper comes in the afternoon and is home when the kids arrive from school. Despite the importance of a career to her, this woman believes in marriage and its importance, too.

"I enjoy marriage or I wouldn't be married. I don't need it for economic reasons. And with all their activities my children are hardly ever home. I think they too could survive very well with one parent. Why do I choose marriage? I don't like to live alone without another adult, and I don't like to keep changing partners. Marriage gives me a sense of warmth, a feeling of being loved, a feeling of having taken out an option on a partnership which I greatly enjoy. If I just lived with my husband outside of marriage, that would indicate to me that he was okay for a while but I'd soon be moving on to other things. That may have been right for me when I was in my twenties but now I've other things to think about. I'm very involved in my work and I'm basically content, now that I've found a husband I admire and love, to stay with him. I like the nesting instinctual feeling that pervades the house, and I look forward to getting home every evening and sharing my experience with the same person.

"But I'm human. I sometimes think about having an affair or wonder what it would be like with someone else. I remain attracted to other men. But a lot of life is a game and I realize I don't have the time to play all the angles. I may lose out on adventure, but having found a man who is right for me on the second try, I gain in mutual companionship. It's comforting to know that there are things we both enjoy and we do not have to be forever spending time learning to know each other, finding out what the other person is like. All the elementary efforts have long ago been made. Continual newness can be tiring. We feel so close that often we say the same thing at the same moment, even though the subject hasn't been brought up. That's a good feeling, too. And there are so many things we don't have to say because we know them. There are assets we can accumulate and pride we can take in each other's work.

"We have a good marriage, so neither of us feels trapped. When marriage is good it can be very, very good. Great fun. Sensing that you are very close to another human being can in itself be just as exciting as making new conquests. It's rare to be able to match so perfectly and when you do, you don't think too seriously or for too long of living in any other way. The sense of belonging to something together, a common thing that you have created and made strong and which comforts you, this thing which is your marriage, is delightfully fulfilling. I can see living with my husband without marriage just as easily, but it leaves all the doors open. To me it would signify a looser relationship. I see taking the step of getting married as firming up an agreement, as we do in business. Few agreements here are verbal, and the commitment of a written agreement gives the businessman or the wife and husband a sense of security, not necessarily financial, but emotional as well. All contracts are not bad *per se.* I don't see any reason to destroy the marriage contract. I would like to see it become something that is more businesslike, more easily broken or rearranged as circumstances change.

"I suppose marriage is thinking that I'm always going to have the one adult in the world I love more than any other. And I like that feeling, even though marriages don't always last. We enjoy our sex, though I'm sure we don't have it as often as someone who is not married and is moving from person to person. We enjoy our evenings, our vacations, and we make time for our children. Perhaps one's appreciation of a marriage contract depends on how busy the rest of your life is, how committed to work your days are. If you aren't very revved up by your work, a more exciting personal life might be more necessary. But if you are busy and involved, the excitement is of a different kind. You have it all day long, and you don't need it on the personal level. You just want to relax in your marriage and enjoy it. Which I do."

Why Second Marriages Can Fail

In the first case the woman's marriage may not last. She may not want it to. What makes a marriage work is almost indefinable. You can attribute success to mutual interests, experience, wisdom, love, sharing, caring, and all the positive combinations that two people can create, but that may not be enough to explain it. Part of what makes a marriage work or fail may be within the person, involving inner needs and drives that neither he nor she can understand, profound chemistries that defy analysis, subtleties that tip the balance. Or it may be ridiculous superficialities, such as looks and smells and the sound of a voice or a laugh. Such elusive elements in a marriage remind me of the fellow who would date a girl once and then never take her out again. Despairing that he would go unmarried, his friends asked for a list of all the requirements he wanted in his ideal girl: eyes, hair, interests, and so on. He compiled the list, they found the girl, and he dated her. But that also was the end of it. He never asked her out again. His friends wanted to know what was wrong this time. He said quite simply: "Yes, she had the right color eyes and hair and the same interests as mine, but I just didn't like her."

There are other reasons for the breakup of a second marriage that are easier to explain, such as the obvious fact that not everyone is going to grow up as soon, or in the same direction, or perhaps ever. Though this is less likely to be a problem the second time, it still happens. A woman in her early thirties whose second marriage also ended in divorce admitted: "I know I messed up my two marriages because I just matured late. I was a late bloomer. It wasn't that I was slow to learn from my mistakes, I just hadn't even waked up yet. I went sailing through life without even looking at where I was going. I didn't understand myself any better when I married the second time than I had the first time. It took two mistakes frosted with a bit of age to jolt me into learning about myself."

It is true that most people seem to learn enough about themselves after a first marriage to prevent making the same mistake again. But there's no guarantee that everyone will, and there are those people who never do. No one is infallible. Some who didn't show good judgment the first time won't the second time. Some will need three marriages to find the right partner and some will begin to suspect that they are not the sort who should be married at all because they are too independent or too unstable.

One remarried man realized this when he told me: "We are thinking about separating. I lead an unscheduled life. I used to think the tension was from my second wife. But now I think it's from the fact that I may not be cut out for marriage."

Second marriages can end because of neurosis, psychosis, alcoholism, illness, or other such catastrophes that are completely unpredictable and may erode the union beyond endurance. Cruel accidents of fate can cause an otherwise happy person to slip into a difficult neurosis. Another woman whose second marriage ended told me that her husband had lost quite a bit of money in the stock market and became more and more difficult to live with. "It wasn't that he lost his money that mattered," she said, "it was that without money he was a different person. He began to believe that people at work didn't like him any more, didn't give him credit for things he did. He was depressed all the time and drank too much. Every night he bathed himself in self-pity and never went to bed before two in the morning. I was becoming a mental and physical wreck. Finally he found a woman he liked and who looked up to him, someone much younger than I. That was all his ego needed. A shot in the arm to keep him going. That's why my second marriage broke up, and I was ready to kill myself over being left. Can you imagine wanting to go on that way? Now I realize it's the greatest thing that could have happened to me. I don't blame myself for having had two failures. People aren't perfect. They're not machines. Things go wrong with people the first time, and they can go wrong for the same reasons or other reasons the second time. There are moments when I don't think people should try to stay together for more than ten years. It's asking too much of a relationship."

Second marriages can collapse because the couple may have had too many children, have perhaps already had too many in their first marriage, and can't take the bombardment of so many egos. However, the problems of too many children and the strains of a suddenly lowered income don't seem to be the main cause of second failures. With everyone trying harder and with a time limit on the situation as kids grow older, most second divorces (which occur on the average at ages thirty-eight for women and forty-one for men) are likely to be caused by permanent immaturity, psychiatric problems, or creative needs which preclude certain people's ever finding life tolerable with just one or two others.

A second marriage may also come to a halt because that marriage can just go on too long and wear itself thin. To expect two people, even in a second marriage, to endure forever with precisely the same momentum and in the same direction is expecting a lot, though they obviously have a better chance than when they were young and inexperienced. A woman told me quite candidly why her second marriage ended: "I think it had gotten old and worn out. We had been married for thirteen years and that's a long time. I think marriages as well as people grow old, become flaccid, wrinkled, sick, tired. We knew each other too well, and although that can be good and comforting, it can also be boring. Everything was predictable," she said. "And because he knew what I would always do and I knew what he would always say, how he would react to things, we began to irritate each other. The same problems, the same reactions, the same petty annoyances continue to repeat themselves after a while. A couple can go through just so much that is new. By the time six or seven years have gone by, you've seen it all and heard it all before. Even if you get along and still like each other, you might well want to try something and someone different. I think it takes very special kinds of people who can continue on forever. Perhaps they need to be very busy individually as well as even-tempered."

She told me that she had remarried and was living with her third husband. "It's great this time, because I have a career and that makes all the difference. It makes us behave more like equals, it keeps us more interested in each other, it gives me the right to complain about certain things, assert myself the way I felt I couldn't do when my former husbands were earning all the money and running everything."

If the time comes, as it so often does for people who have been in and out of a first marriage, when they have learned enough about themselves and know what they as individuals need to be happy and know how to get along with another person on an intimate level, then a marriage—first, second, or third—may work. But the marriage needs to be big enough and flexible enough to leave room for the shrinking and expanding that come with social change and with age. If the marriage is not flexible, if the people within it can't agree on issues they thought were understood, or on the new elements that constantly come up where big policy decisions have to be made, then second marriage is vulnerable. To expect all second marriages to be perfect is as childish as expecting all first marriages to succeed.

But I think that as people in the future become more adventuresome, less influenced by the childhood memory of what their parents thought was right, as they become more interested in the number of options an adult life can encompass, there will be more divorces instead of fewer. More second marriages will end, and people will move on to the next situation. They will not see divorce the second time as something to fear or as a sign of instability (though for some people it may well be) but as an accepted line of demarcation between the past and the future, just as we see graduation from grade school, high school, and college, or moving up from one job to the next. More second marriages will also end for the same reason that more first marriages will end. There is increasingly less social pressure to prevent them, and those who would have stuck out a second mistake (what would neighbors and family think of not one but two divorces!) will no longer do so.

Thoughts about Kids

In the future it is doubtful that most women will sacrifice their career interests to stay at home and raise children the way their parents did. More people are saying that they do not want children, some are even regretting having had them, and it is probable that those who plan to have children in the future will have them later. I was told: "When I look at my kids, I can't imagine not having them. But I should have waited," and "Hold off having the kids and get to know each other."

A woman freely admitted: "When I had kids I realized this is not what it's cracked up to be. Walking kids around the park, getting my toes in the sand. I will counsel my girls not to marry when they are too young. How old should they be? Between twenty-four and fifty, whenever they have their heads together. And they should think twice about having children." Nothing is automatic any more. When couples have children at later ages, they will inevitably have fewer and remarriage will not be overweighted with as many children as many second marriages have been. This should certainly make it easier on everyone.

It is the opinion of many people that children don't need one exclusive mother and father all day or one nuclear family for all their years at home. There are different options; one does not have to have all the kids, all at home, all the time, all of them stepping on each other's toes and sensibilities.

New Ideas

At times there is a kind of uncomfortable, ill-at-ease feeling in the way many who are in first and second marriages sense their particular situations. Things don't always quite fit right. Everyone is squirming and shoving to make room, but it's hard to squeeze present concepts into the shape of the future. And it's hard to fit new life-styles—kids, careers, remarriage—into old molds. There is a feeling among many people I talked to that we need new institutions to accommodate our new images of marriage.

Margaret Mead, who seems never at a loss for new ideas, suggests that "We badly need to recognize a new form of marriage—a marriage between childless partners with no commitment to continuity. Such marriages should be easier to contract, should involve no automatic economic relationships, and should be capable of dissolution by mutual consent without undue delay, cost, or supervision from the constituted organs of society. On the other hand, marriages which are parental should be placed in a different category; the couple should understand what a marriage with children is—a lifelong relationship which will end only with death."*

The idea of two separate types of marriages is interesting and the two kinds of relationships are certainly different enough to require different kinds of contracts. Since many people might contract to live together without children for quite a few years before having a child, it would be necessary for them to sign new contracts when they decide to have children. They would have to marry the same person twice, but differently. First a personal marriage and later on, a parental marriage. Divorce in either case would of course be possible; but it would be more difficult when children are involved and people might therefore take a parental marriage much more seriously.

It seems certain that in the future there will no longer be one type of marriage. There will be many kinds of marriage, many options, many arrangements, many different choices from conventional marriage to parental marriage, to open marriage in which both have affairs, to a just-living-together marriage (which might be called a singles marriage), even to group marriage, or almost any other arrangement you can think of. There will be multiple choices, and a person will be able to pick one of the possibilities and stay with it forever or choose several possibilities, moving from one to another as he grows older. This is really what we are trying to do today when we have one kind of marriage at first, then one with children, and then perhaps divorce and still another marriage. In the future we will be more conscious of these shifts and will arrange them more deliberately as our contracts begin and end, when each of our phases begin and end. Even where marriage to one person seems to be lasting, it may

*Margaret Mead, "Anomalie in American Postdivorce Relationships," in *Divorce and After,* ed. Paul Bohannan (Garden City, N.Y.: Doubleday Anchor Books, 1971), pp. 123–24.

be a good idea for the couple to have to renew their contract every five years, as has so often been suggested, simply to make the termination of marriage automatic (if it ends every five years, one doesn't have to go to the ridiculous expense of ending it by divorce), and to keep marginally unhappy people from just dragging along out of laziness or fear.

Dr. Weitzman sees the future of marriage moving toward a pattern of serial monogamy. This means that we will stay with just one person in each phase of life and then move on to the next person in the next phase, much like a continuing soap opera. There will be the formation of new families, says Dr. Weitzman, throughout the life cycle. There will be greater diversity in the functions and purposes of marriage. She says: "Some will want to raise kids, others will not; some will focus on shared leisure activities, others on work or a career; some of the new families will last twenty or forty years; others for two or three years; some will want to build a total life together, others will be limited relationships in which spouses will decide to share a period such as graduate school or working in a foreign country, raising small kids, etc." She points out, as have others, that because couples live longer they have much more time ahead of them and the stage at which they are no longer taking active care of children, the postparental stage, is a brand-new phenomenon in human history. She says that "People did not live long enough in the past to reach it. Some believe the human race has never been mature enough for enduring marriages, a fact obscured by early deaths."

It is probably true that, for most people, a fifty-year marriage that remains healthy, interesting, lively, and continually challenging is an impossibility. As we pass through stages from childhood into adolescence, into young adulthood, and then mature adulthood, we reach a point where another thirty years still lies ahead which calls for new relationships. Now that the moral injunctions of the past have faded, there are many possibilities, many ways to go, many kinds of marriage to look for and agree on. As life gets longer because we live longer, it seems to feel shorter because there is so much more opportunity and so many more things to do. We are clearly in a period of questioning old social rules which we have always taken as immutable, never to be challenged. We are searching for new formulas that will give freedom to our potential development.

When I think back on my own three marriages, I realize now that in my own innocence, ignorance, and fear of being told by society that I was out-of-step, I was seeking something new. Even before the 1970s, when such ideas broke out into the open, I was trying to fit a need within me into whatever constraints convention allowed. My first marriage was carefree, began in college, memorable. It influenced me in many ways, and it was short-lived. Then came the next phase, a marriage of travel, living abroad, and aiding someone whose career had a better start than mine. I did not switch partners as the next phase of childbearing came, though I might well have. This was a period of settling down and constructing a life that a child could fit into. In my third marriage, it's a different time again, one of pursuing an independent career and at times working closely with someone else, while in a few years my son will be off to college. Had I begun my adult life in the 1970s, I might have made other choices, but even so, my response to change in my own life was evident.

Among other new ideas is the suggestion, offered by almost everyone I interviewed, that people who think they want to be married should live together before marrying—the opposite advice of what parents traditionally have taught children. Some go as far as to say that living together for at least two years should be compulsory before any marriage is allowed.

Included in the new concepts of the state we call marriage is a relationship which one man envisioned. The couple would continue to enjoy friendships with both men and women, single and married. "We don't have in mind the cliché of 'open marriage' with freewheeling coitus among friends. But we do believe in maintaining friendship with former lovers, and in friends of both sexes. We are consciously opposing the cultural stereotypes of 'Mister-and-Missus' having to do everything inseparably and together with other safe couples. We also oppose the stereotype of the wife being totally dependent on the male (the man she lives with or her husband) for all her friendship values."

It has been suggested by some that we have marital sabbaticals or vacations from our marriages during which we can learn more about others, refresh our viewpoints, come back to the relationship filled with new experience with which to enrich it.

A woman thought that marriage might be more successful if the members of the couple kept separate houses or apartments and simply were together for part of their time. The separateness might make for a more mature interaction. "I think living together all the time," she said, "makes too many people lapse into the problems and habits of the home they grew up in and the marriage becomes more of a mother-son relationship, where she is always taking care of him and he is demanding and spoiled. Marriage the way we live it feels too irrevocably permanent, and anything that permanent becomes a trap."

People are looking for new ways of living with kids in less traumatic conditions. Someone advised having the children and then turning them over to someone else after puberty. "We need a young adult-raising agency (not a boarding school) after age eleven or thirteen when they want their independence but the parents can't support it, and it leads to conflict. They are hell until they are independent. They really ought to live somewhere else, some kind of mid-station between total dependence on parents and the independence of college."

And a new kind of custody arrangement has been suggested for parents who divorce. Instead of splitting custody and having the children live with each parent part of the time, one couple got an apartment for the kids where the kids always stayed and then each parent moved in for a six-month period and then out again as the other parent arrived. This looks like an ingenious, if expensive, solution to the problem of bouncing kids back and forth between two sets of friends, schools, and homes.

A teacher in Oregon has devised a new course he calls "Contemporary Living," in which students go through simulated marriages with plastic rings, and then through the motions of finding apartments; developing family budgets; buying furniture if they can afford it; looking for jobs; making compromises; learning their responsibilities; making decisions; discussing utility bills, car insurance, life insurance; and going over the things they might have to give up to have a baby. At the end of the course, each student couple is required to go through a mock divorce with all its attendant agonies. More education of this kind which deflates the glamour of marriage and makes it into something real—with dollars, disappointments, mothers-in-law, babies, and unpaid gas bills—will probably appear in the future in high schools.

And there are those who are at work on devising tests which would help people select the right marriage partner to begin with and bring together men and women with a higher probability of having a successful marriage.

In a recent survey on the quality of life, conducted by three University of Michigan sociologists, the people interviewed rated good health and a happy marriage as the two most important values. If this kind of yardstick is used, it must mean that the excellence of life has dropped considerably, for certain diseases, such as cancer, are on the increase, and that signal of unhappy marriages known as divorce has certainly increased. It should be stressed that although most people see divorce as a sign of some dread cancer in their relationship, more and more people are beginning to see it as a first sign of repair or cure after the disease hits.

Future Trends

People often talk about whether, because of the current state of affairs, it's a good time in history to be alive. Well, events often stall on the political and international front, but on the domestic side, it's an exciting and fast-moving time to be alive. Without denying the importance of marriage in our society, one cannot help wondering if we are not witnessing the first signs of an overhaul in marriage customs that may lead to greater freedom in the relationships between men and women. We may be living through and helping to create a new concept of marriage, one of those quantum leaps in knowledge and experience that is like the invention of the telescope. Whole new worlds open up. Society has begun to legitimize the many possible ways in which people can relate to one another all through life. Our behavior patterns have changed even before the social scientists have had a chance to analyze them. The way it was in the 1960s is no longer the way it is in the 1970s.

Sweden, for example, is a country that has anticipated many trends in Western society in recent years, from modern furniture to socialized medicine. In that country a revolution in marriage styles is already under way. In the nine years between 1966 and 1975, the rate for first marriages fell 30 per cent, the divorce rate increased 135 per cent. The rate for second marriages also fell drastically, while the illegitimacy rate rose. This apparent disenchantment with conventional marriage is emerging in the other Scandinavian countries as well. With more divorces and fewer marriages, it simply means that more and more people are staying single, living together rather than marrying, or marrying late.

It's not only in more socially avant-garde countries that one senses this radical change in family and marriage patterns. It has recently been reported that in Brazil, the largest Roman Catholic country in the world, where divorce is against legal and religious codes, thousands of unhappily married people are getting legal separations and then entering into illegal second marriages. According to the account, ". . . illegal second marriages have become an accepted part of life among the middle and upper classes. . . ." Amusingly enough, these "marriages" are written up in social columns and there is little social stigma attached to them. There seems to be the same drive toward marital freedom and experimentation in two of the most opposite countries imaginable.

And in the United States, not only has the divorce rate been rising with one out of three marriages ultimately ending in divorce, but among women in the twenty- to twenty-four-year age bracket, a period when most of them traditionally marry, the proportion of those remaining single rose from 28 per cent in 1960 to 40 per cent in 1975. American women are postponing marriage. Why? For one thing, there are more women in college. Twice as many women were enrolled in college in 1975 as in 1965. Second, there are more women than men in the traditional age range. This phenomenon, called the "marriage squeeze," came about because girls born during the baby-boom years reached marriageable age two or three years before the men born during the same period. Third, there has been an increase in opportunity for women to work. And, last, the women's movement has kept women from jumping into the housewife role quite so eagerly. They now look forward to traveling, studying, working, having experience and not committing themselves to someone right away. No one knows what fraction of the women who have postponed marriage will in fact marry. Very often when you postpone things, you never get around to doing them. Bachelors traditionally enjoy their freedom and, similarly, these women may become accustomed to their lifestyles and decide never to change them. Perhaps they think the spontaneous affection they find in living with another person without contracts (which can be broken), without promises (which may not be kept), and without children (which can be encumbering) could not be sustained with marriage. Perhaps they are afraid of the routine and rut of marriage they have seen in their parents' lives, and are not willing to settle for this kind of future. Perhaps they don't feel the pressure to marry and have children right away because they don't want children right away, and maybe not at all. Their mothers, anxiously waiting to become grandmothers and relive the sweetness of motherhood will have to wait.

Unlike what has occurred in a country like India, our women do not have to bear children in large numbers to ensure that some will survive to support them in their old age. We have been able to control infant diseases and their mortality rate. Women today are also sensitive to growing food shortages throughout the world. They know children are expensive (costing as much as $100,000 from birth through college), and they make a varied life-style more difficult. So they cling to their options, their independence, their work, their friends, their lovers. They do not rush into marriage and look for exorbitantly expensive apartments with cross-ventilation and lots of closets and lots of furniture to be dusted and rugs to be vacuumed. They think of developing their potential, of esteeming themselves as people. The days of women as breeding machines, once needed to guarantee the continuance of the family name and fortune, are over.

Today's family is shrinking and becoming compact, like our cars. It is thus more easily mobile and better able to enjoy the leisure of greater affluence. Among women aged twenty to twenty-four who have been married, only 24 per cent were childless in 1960; in 1975, 43 per cent—almost half—of women in this same age range were still childless. Again the same thing might be said about childbearing as was said about marriage. With more couples putting off having children, a large number may well decide to postpone them permanently as other opportunities arise and they keep getting older.

So the future shape of family life looks as though more men and women will stay single longer, and will put off having children, maybe permanently. And more will tackle a series of life-style options. Living together before marriage (perhaps replacing marriage) seems to be the one thing that everyone wants. Cohabitation is the fastest growing life-style in the United States among young adults. An increasing number of men and women are sharing their quarters with an unrelated partner of the opposite sex. As more young people stay single and maintain their own households, there are also, because of divorce and separation, more single-parent families headed by women, and more children living with only one parent. The number of households headed by single people doubled between 1970 and 1975. The single scene is growing.

In June 1975 the U.S. Census Bureau, which has become increasingly imaginative and investigative under the influence of Dr. Paul Glick, did a study of the marital history of men and women. Here are some of the encapsulated results, the latest figures which help to clarify the image of our marital future:

—First of all, and quite surprisingly, high divorce rates are not the result of the mid-life crisis which hits so many people when they begin to see the specter of old age and death around the corner and wonder whether they have gotten all they want out of life. A greater amount of divorce has occurred among the young, in spite of their shorter period of marriage. Almost half those whose first marriage ends in divorce are in their twenties. The average age of first divorce is twenty-seven for women and twenty-nine for men.

—There is also no evidence, according to the Census Bureau, that there is an increase in divorce after the children have grown up. This probably means that a lot of people who stick out a bad marriage and intend to wait till the kids leave home before divorcing are just deluding themselves. They will, in many instances, just never get around to it; they won't bother.

—Although about one-third of recent first marriages will probably end in divorce, most people are divorced only once.

—Among those who get a first divorce, four out of five people eventually remarry. This includes five out of every six men and not quite as many, or three out of every four, women. Those who are widowed are less likely to remarry than divorced people.

—Slightly more second than first marriages will end in divorce, but most will succeed. The projection is that about 40 per cent of second marriages of people in their late twenties and early thirties will end in divorce.

—Only a small fraction of people who have ever been married marry more than twice, though Census experts believe this figure may increase as people become less inhibited.

—The most typical age for remarriage is twenty-five to thirty-four for men and twenty to twenty-nine for women.

—Although there is an excess of women in the marriage market now because of the "marriage squeeze," the situation is changing.

Because the birth rate has declined sharply during the last fifteen years, a reverse marriage squeeze will develop by 1985 and last for about ten years. During this time there will be about 5 per cent more men than women in the ages when people usually marry. This would make it appear that from around 1985 to 2000, women will have a larger choice of men to pick from if they want to find a man to live with or marry, and it just may make them more demanding and more fickle, as men have been able to be.

—Several basic future trends pointed out in the Census report are: the delayed entry into marriage of women; the shorter average length of time between marriages; and, as we have seen, the divorcing of more couples, and the establishing of new families with different partners. Divorce and remarriage or singleness seem to be the new direction.

Underlying all our difficulties with marriage has certainly been a desire for freer, more realistic and equal relationships, unfettered by traditional legal contracts. It has been proposed that all we may really need is a contract between a man and a woman who decide to have a child, agreeing to support it equally until it reaches twenty-one, regardless of what either may do thereafter or how many marriage-like liaisons they may form with others.

A Princeton University sociologist whom I interviewed offered this view of the future of marriage in America: "I think we are lagging behind Sweden by six or seven years," he said. "Though more people here will stay single, we will probably not have as precipitous a decline in our marriage rate as in Sweden. My guess is that in the next decade, Americans will marry later in life. But marriage won't disappear. There are too many entanglements and economic considerations and the complication of children to keep it going. Women are not yet sufficiently independent economically to undermine the institution completely."

Our remarried people of today are, I believe, the pioneers who have had to break new ground, largely unaided, without traditions and signposts to guide them. For remarrying people in the future, it will all be easier and less complex for everyone, as they will have a better understanding of what is happening, why they behave as they do, and what to expect. Remarriage, of course, may be only the first step in an eventual total breakaway from marriage. It is entirely likely that after experimenting and trying a series of new possibilities, marriage will be supplanted someday, either by some other form of living together or not even living together, but just relating when it is desired.

For the moment, however, the high rate of remarriage in America indicates that we still believe in marriage in some form. At the same time we seem to be more tolerant of people who depart from the accepted patterns of the past. Our attitudes are broadening toward other life-styles, including second marriages—for those who can't or don't wish to maintain the traditional first marriage. For quite some time to come, and for an ever-growing number of people, remarriage will probably mean a second chance to find the good life.

INDEX

National Fertility Study, 126
Neurosis and divorce, 157

Parents:
favoritism and, 108
guilt feelings of, 86
opposition to remarriage, 54
overindulgence of children by, 86–87
prospective spouses as parents, 85. *See also* Stepparents
visits, frequency of, 103
Parmet, Belle, 3–4
Physical attractiveness and marriage, 17
Post, Emily, 62–63
Privacy, lack of, 76–77

Remarriage:
changed social atmosphere and, 141
children and, 98–120
community pressures and, 37
contractual safeguards, 61–62
dissimilarity of new partners to former, 33–34
duration of, 6
economic security and, 122, 37–38
education and, 5
effect on children, 74–77
greater effort expended on, 140
greater realism in, 34, 132
happiness and, 123–25
honesty of partners, 130
improvement over former marriage, 121–22
income and, 5
informality of, 1–2
jealousy and, 46–49
lack of competitiveness in, 131

in literature, 70
maturity and, 157
need for commitment and, 35
new criteria for, 32–33
reasons for, 34–37
scarcity of information about, 4, 10
sex and, 125–30
renewed ambitions and, 95
rate, 3
shared interests and, 137–38
statistics, 168–69
tolerance and, 133–34
traditional values and, 38
unsuccessful, 153–54. *See also* Divorce.
Rockefeller, Nelson, 7
Romantic love, 17

Sex:
cohabitation and, 127
extramarital, 128
frequency studies, 126
premarital, survey of, 128
remarriage and, 125–30
as taboo subject, 12
privacy and, 76–77
Spock, Jane, 6, 38
Stepchildren:
adaptation of, 93
addressing stepparents, 67–69, 105, 106
backgrounds of, 80–81
as bonds in new marriages, 96–97
challenges to childless stepparent, 97
eating habits, 89–90
guilt feelings, 72
idealization of natural parents, 80–81
insecurity of, 87